**Grade 1**

 SCHOLA

MW01196367

Reading & Math Practice

200 Teacher-Approved Practice Pages to Build Essential Skills

New York • Toronto • London • Auckland • Sydney
Mexico City • New Delhi • Hong Kong • Buenos Aires

Teaching *Resources*

Contents

Cover design: Scott Davis
Interior design: Adrienne Downey, Melinda Belter, and Sydney Wright
Interior illustrations: Teresa Anderko, Melinda Belter, Maxie Chambliss, Kate Flanagan, Rusty Fletcher, Mike Gordon,
James Graham Hale, Anne Kennedy, Maggie Smith, Sydney Wright, and Bari Weissman © Scholastic Inc.

Image credits: page 84 (left) © Santia/Shutterstock; (right) © Paul Broadbent/Shutterstock; page 108 © Dan Barnes/
iStockphoto; page 164 used by permission of A de F, Ltd., © 1995; page 188 © rosta/iStockphoto

ISBN: 978-0-545-67257-3
Written by Marcia Miller and Martin Lee.
Copyright © 2014 by Scholastic Inc.
All rights reserved. Printed in the U.S.A.
Published by Scholastic Inc.

1 2 3 4 5 6 7 8 9 10   14   21 20 19 18 17 16 15 14

Introduction

Welcome!

Reading & Math Practice: Grade 1 is the perfect way to support the learning your child needs to soar in school and beyond. The colorful, fun, and engaging activity pages in this book will give your child plenty of opportunities to practice the important reading and math skills first graders are expected to master. These teacher-approved practice pages are a great way to help your child:

- ☑ reinforce key academic skills and concepts
- ☑ meet curriculum standards
- ☑ prepare for standardized tests
- ☑ succeed in school
- ☑ become a lifelong learner!

Research shows that independent practice helps children gain mastery of essential skills. Each set of practice pages contains a collection of activities designed to review and reinforce a range of skills and concepts. The consistent format will help your child work independently and with confidence. Skills include:

Reading & Language Arts	Math
Phonics	Place Value & Number Sense
Vocabulary	Addition & Subtraction
Handwriting Practice	Logic & Critical Thinking
Reading Comprehension	Solving Word Problems
Early Grammar & Spelling	Interpreting Charts & Graphs

Turn the page for information about how these exercises will help your child meet the College and Career Readiness Standards for reading, language, and mathematics. Page 5 offers suggestions for introducing the practice pages to your child along with helpful tips for making the experience go smoothly. Pages 6–9 provide a close-up look at the features in each set of practice pages.

We hope you enjoy doing the activities in this book with your child. Your involvement will help make this a valuable educational experience and will support and enhance your child's learning!

Connections to the College and Career Readiness Standards

The standards for College and Career Readiness (CCR) serve as the backbone for the practice pages in this book. These broad standards were developed to establish educational expectations meant to provide students nationwide with a quality education that prepares them for college and careers. The following lists show how the activities in this book align with the standards in key areas of focus for students in grade 1.

Standards for English Language Arts	Standards for Mathematics
Reading Standards (Literary and Informational Texts)	**Mathematical Practice**
• Key Ideas and Details	1. Make sense of problems and persevere in solving them.
• Craft and Structure	2. Reason abstractly and quantitatively.
• Integration of Knowledge and Ideas	3. Construct viable arguments and critique the reasoning of others.
• Range of Reading Level and Text Complexity	4. Model with mathematics.
	5. Use appropriate tools strategically.
Foundational Skills	6. Attend to precision.
• Phonics and Word Recognition	7. Look for and make use of structure.
• Fluency	8. Look for and express regularity in repeating reasoning.
Language	**Mathematical Content**
• Conventions of Standard English	• Operations & Algebraic Thinking
• Knowledge of Language	• Number & Operations in Base Ten
• Vocabulary Acquisition and Use	• Measurement & Data
	• Geometry

Reading & Math Practice, Grade 1 © 2014 Scholastic Inc.

Getting Started

Each practice packet consists of two double-sided pages—one for reading followed by one for math. Introduce the packet to your child by going through the directions and walking through its features. Point out that activities in each section focus on different kinds of skills, and that the same features repeat throughout, always in the same order and position. In general, the practice pages progress in difficulty level and build on skills covered on previous pages. See pages 6–9 for more information.

Helpful Tips

★ For ease of use, gently tear out the pages your child will be working on along the perforated edges.

★ Invite your child to complete each packet over the course of a week, doing two or three exercises on a practice page each day.

★ If desired, allow your child to choose the order in which he or she will complete the exercises on the practice pages.

★ You'll find an answer key for each practice page, beginning on page 211. Review the answers together and encourage your child to share the thinking behind his or her answers.

★ Support your child's efforts and offer help when needed.

★ Display your child's work and share his or her progress with family and friends!

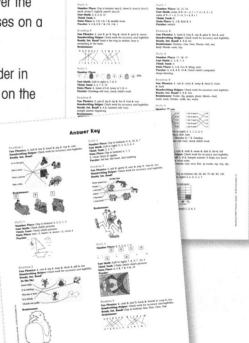

A Close-Up Look at the Practice Pages

Each of the double-sided reading practice pages includes the following skill-building features.

Reading (Side A)

Fun Phonics The first feature on Side A focuses on a key phonics or word-study topic. For some children, this activity may provide review. Other learners may need more support or hints to help them succeed.

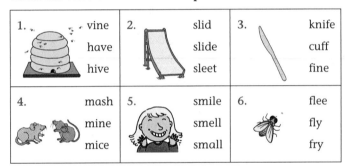

Reading 21
Side A

FUN Phonics

Circle the word that names each picture.

1.	vine	2.	slid	3.	knife
	have		slide		cuff
	hive		sleet		fine
4.	mash	5.	smile	6.	flee
	mine		smell		fly
	mice		small		fry

Handwriting Helper

✎ Trace. Then write.

Inez

James

Kent

Lynn

Handwriting Helper This exercise offers your child a chance to practice manuscript handwriting. The words and phrases include practice in writing both lower- and uppercase letters.

Reading (Side B)

Ready, Set, Read! Side B begins with a brief fiction or nonfiction reading passage, followed by text-based questions. Tell your child to read the passage first and then answer the questions. Demonstrate how to fill in the circles for multiple-choice questions. For questions that require writing, provide an additional sheet of paper, if needed.

📖 Ready, Set, READ!

Read. Then answer the questions.

Can It Jump?

Ask an egg to jump. It cannot.
Pick up an egg and put it down.
That is not a jump.
Roll the egg. It can roll.
But that is still not a jump.
AHA! An egg has no legs.
So an egg cannot jump.

1. Why can't an egg jump?

_____

2. AHA! means
   ○ A. Oh, no!   ○ B. Oh, I know!

🌀 BrainTeaser 🌀

Read and draw.

- a fish in the water
- a bird by the cloud
- a smile on the sun

92

Brainteaser Side B concludes with an entertaining word or language challenge: a puzzle, code, riddle, or other engaging task designed to stretch the mind. Encourage your child to tease out tricky solutions.

Math (Side A)

Number Place The first feature on Side A reviews place-value and number-sense skills related to whole numbers, counting, and groupings in tens and ones.

Number Place

Count. Circle groups of 10. Write how many.

☆ ☆	☆ ☆
_____ tens _____ ones	_____ tens _____ ones

FAST Math

Subtract. Think about doubles.

$14 - 7 =$ _____ $18 - 9 =$ _____ $12 - 6 =$

$20 -$ _____ $= 10$ $16 -$ _____ $= 8$ $10 -$ _____

Fast Math This activity addresses computation skills with the goal of building automaticity, fluency, and accuracy.

💡 Think Tank

Jalal collects magnets. He has 8 magnets of animals. He has 9 magnets of boats. How many magnets does Jalal have? He has

_____ magnets.

Show your work in the tank.

Think Tank This feature offers a word problem that draws from a wide spectrum of grade-appropriate skills, strategies, and approaches. In the think tank itself, your child can draw, do computations, and work out his or her thinking.

85

& Math Practice, Grade 1 © 2014 Scholastic Inc.

Reading & Math Practice, Grade 1 © 2014 Scholastic Inc.

Math (Side B)

> **Data Place** In this section, your child solves problems based on reading, collecting, representing, and interpreting data that is presented in many formats: lists, tables, charts, pictures, and, especially, graphs.

Data Place

Use the grid to answer the questions.

1. To find ●, start at 0.

   Go **across** _____ and then **up** _____ .

2. To find ▲, start at 0.

   Go **across** _____ and then **up** _____ .

3. To find ■, start at 0.

   Go **across** _____ and then **up** _____ .

4. Go **across** 1 and then **up** 3.

   Draw an **X**.

Puzzler

Figure out each pattern.
Write what comes next.

1 — 2 — 1 — 3 — 1 — 4 — ○ — ○ — ○

4 — 14 — 24 — 34 — 44 — 54 — ○ — ○ — ○

3 — 6 — 9 — 12 — 15 — 18 — 21 — ○ — ○ — ○

10 — 5 — 15 — 10 — 20 — 15 — 25 — ○ — ○ — ○

86

> **Puzzler** Side B always ends with some form of an entertaining challenge: a brainteaser, puzzle, code, or other engaging task designed to stretch the mind.

Reading & Math Practice, Grade 1 © 2014 Scholastic Inc.

FUN Phonics

Name each picture.
Write the letter for the **beginning** sound.

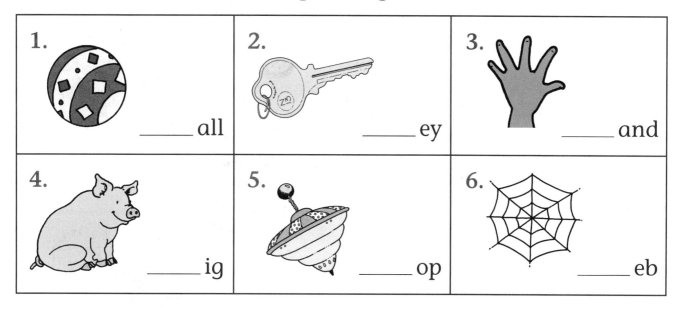

1. _____ all

2. _____ ey

3. _____ and

4. _____ ig

5. _____ op

6. _____ eb

Handwriting Helper

✏️ Trace. Then write.

all

am

and

away

📖 Ready, Set, READ!

Draw lines to match the words and pictures.

Go to the park.

Find a book.

Paint a picture.

Ride a bike.

🌀 BrainTeaser 🌀

Put in order. Write 1, 2, and 3.

Reading & Math Practice, Grade 1 © 2014 Scholastic Inc.

Number Place

Write how many.

🍓	1
🍓🍓🍓🍓	
🍓🍓	

🍓🍓🍓	
🍓	
🍓🍓🍓🍓🍓	

FAST Math

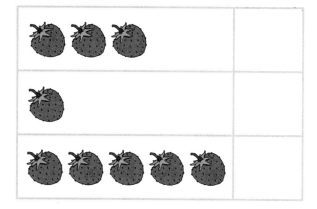

This is a piece of chalk.
Draw a LONGER piece.
Draw a SHORTER piece.

💡 Think Tank

Write your name **inside** the tank.
Write HI **outside** the tank.
Draw ● on the side of the tank.

Data Place

Count .

Count .

Count .

Write how many.

How Many?

 Star	 Heart	 Moon
_____	_____	_____

Which is the most? Circle the number.

Puzzler

Connect the dots.

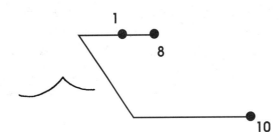

14

Reading & Math Practice, Grade 1 © 2014 Scholastic Inc.

FUN Phonics

Name each picture.
Write the letter for the **beginning** sound.

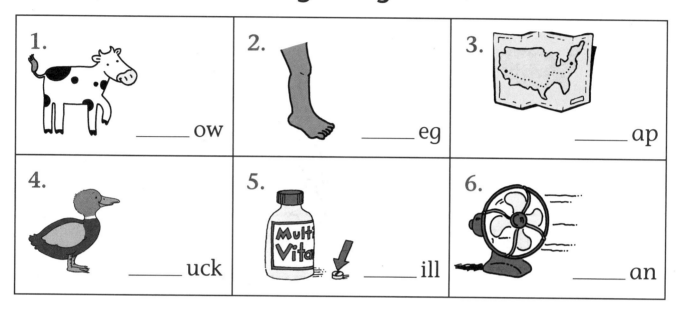

1. _____ ow

2. _____ eg

3. _____ ap

4. _____ uck

5. _____ ill

6. _____ an

Handwriting Helper

✏️ Trace. Then write.

but

big

blue

boys

📖 Ready, Set, READ!

Draw lines to match the words and pictures.

In the Sky

Snow falls.

It is raining.

The sun is hot!

It is windy.

Clouds are puffy.

🌀 BrainTeaser 🌀

Connect the dots in **abc** order.

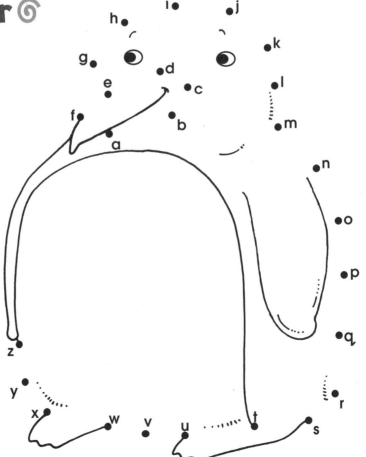

Number Place

Write how many.

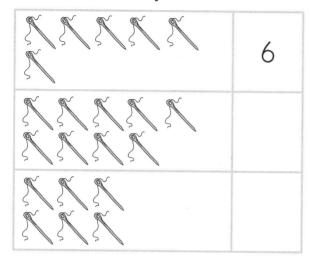

6

FAST Math

Add.

4 + 1 = _____   2 + 3 = _____   1 + 3 = _____

2 + 1 = _____   4 + 2 = _____   3 + 2 = _____

Think Tank

Write the number that is:

under the bowl. _____

in the bowl. _____

over the bowl. _____

next to the bowl. _____

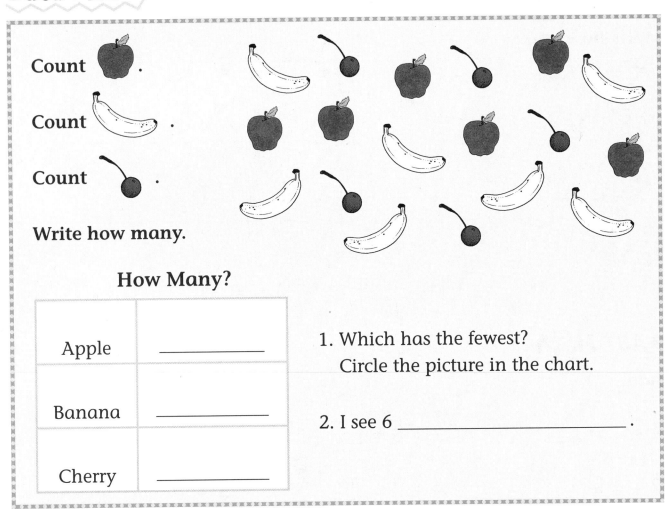

Data Place

Count .

Count .

Count .

Write how many.

How Many?

Apple	_____
Banana	_____
Cherry	_____

1. Which has the fewest?
   Circle the picture in the chart.

2. I see 6 _____ .

Puzzler

X the different one in each row.

FUN Phonics

Name each picture.
Write the letter for the **beginning** sound.

1.  _____ alt	2.  _____ ame	3.  _____ est
4.  _____ eep	5.  _____ ine	6.  _____ oo

Handwriting Helper

✎ Trace. Then write.

cup

can

come

came

📖 Ready, Set, READ!

Draw lines to match the words and pictures.

At the Zoo

Which animal has . . .

humps?

a tall neck?

stripes?

a big mane?

a long trunk?

🌀 BrainTeaser 🌀

Connect the dots in **ABC** order.

20

Number Place

Write the missing numbers.

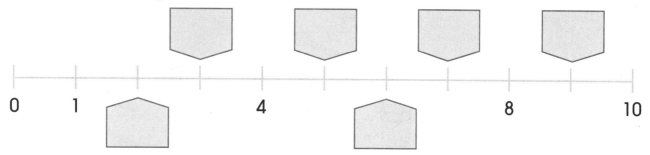

FAST Math

Add.

4 + 3 = _____   5 + 3 = _____   3 + 6 = _____

2 + 5 = _____   4 + 6 = _____   7 + 2 = _____

Think Tank

Hank has these balls. He has 1 less bat. How many bats does Hank have?

In the tank, draw the bats Hank has.

Write the number.

_____

Data Place

Count 🥄 .

Count 🍴 .

Count 🥛 .

Write how many.

1. I count _____ cups.

2. I count _____ forks.

3. I count _____ spoons.

4. One more spoon would make _____ spoons in all.

Puzzler

Count and color.
Use the .

Key	
Number of dots	Color the shape
3	green
4	red
5	blue
6	yellow
7	orange

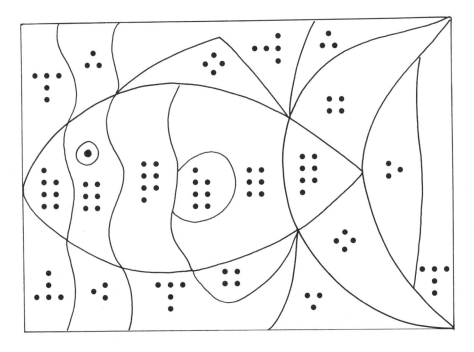

Reading & Math Practice, Grade 1 © 2014 Scholastic Inc.

FUN Phonics

Name each picture.
Write the letter for the **ending** sound.

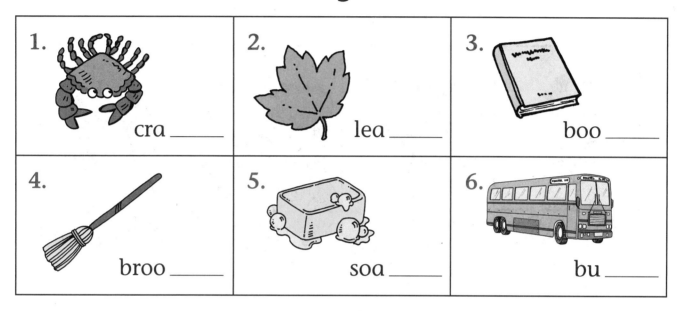

1. cra _____

2. lea _____

3. boo _____

4. broo _____

5. soa _____

6. bu _____

Handwriting Helper

✎ Trace. Then write.

do

did

dips

down

📖 Ready, Set, READ!

Look at the pictures.
Write Tess or Finn to show who does what.

Tess or Finn?

_____ paints the wall.

_____ draws a car.

_____ mops the floor.

_____ reads a book.

🌀 BrainTeaser 🌀

Draw lines to match letter pairs.

A B C D E F G   H I J K L M

d f g b a c e   k l h j m i

Number Place

Draw lines to match words and numbers.

one •	• 4
two •	• 1
three •	• 5
four •	• 2
five •	• 3

six •	• 8
seven •	• 10
eight •	• 7
nine •	• 6
ten •	• 9

FAST Math

Add doubles.

$$\begin{array}{cccccc} & 1 & 2 & 3 & 4 & 5 \\ + & 1 & +\ 2 & +\ 3 & +\ 4 & +\ 5 \\ \hline \\ \hline \end{array}$$

Think Tank

Ann is first in line.
Zack is sixth in line.
How many kids are
between Ann and Zack?

There are _____
kids in between.

**Show your work
in the tank.**

Reading & Math Practice, Grade 1 © 2014 Scholastic Inc.

Data Place

Count the cubes in each train.

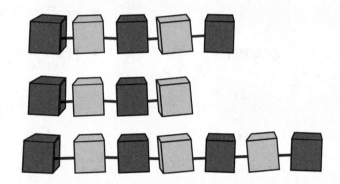

1. How many cubes in the top train? _____

2. How many cubes in the middle train? _____

3. How many cubes in the bottom train? _____

4. Which train is shortest? _____

Puzzler

Add or subtract.
Use the key.

Key

1   2   3   4   5

1. +  = _____

2. + = _____

3. + = _____

4. – = _____

5. –  = _____

6. –  = _____

Reading & Math Practice, Grade 1 © 2014 Scholastic Inc.

FUN Phonics

Name each picture.
Write the letter for the **ending** sound.

1.  coa ____	2. 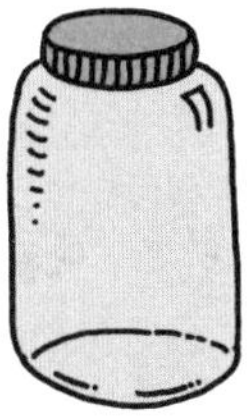 ja ____	3.  fla ____
4.  clou ____	5. 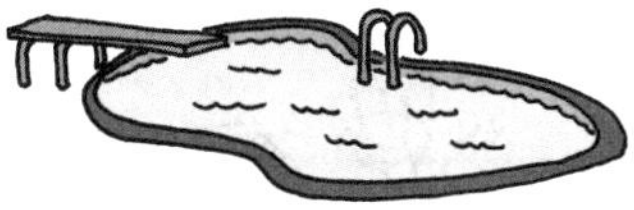 poo ____	6. 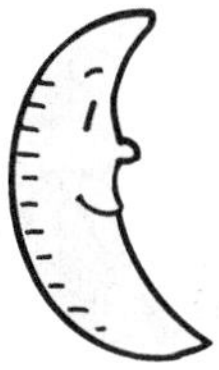 moo ____

Handwriting Helper

✎ Trace. Then write.

find

four

first

funny

📖 Ready, Set, READ!

Read. Then write the names of the frogs in the picture.

Off the Log

Two frogs sit on a log.
"I will hop off," says one.
"I will swim off," says the other.
Hank hops. Suzy swims.
Who is Hank? Who is Suzy?

_____

_____

🌀 BrainTeaser 🌀

Draw lines to match letter pairs.

N O P Q R S T

U V W X Y Z

s r p q t n o

x z v u w y

Reading & Math Practice, Grade 1 © 2014 Scholastic Inc.

Number Place

Follow the directions.

1. Color the **third** jar red.

2. Color the **ninth** jar blue.

3. Color the **sixth** jar green.

4. ✔ the **second** jar.

5. ✗ the **eighth** jar.

6. Write F on the **fourth** jar.

7. Write S on the **seventh** jar.

8. Write 1 on the **first** jar.

9. Write 10 on the **tenth** jar.

10. The _____ jar is empty.

FAST Math

Add.

$1 + 3 + 2 =$ _____

$5 + 2 + 1 =$ _____

$2 + 4 + 1 =$ _____

$3 + 2 + 4 =$ _____

Think Tank

Rico had cards numbered 1 to 10. He left them outside, and they blew away. He found the 5, 1, 8, 3, and 6 cards. Which number cards got lost?

_____

Show your work in the tank.

Data Place

Count the cubes in each tower.
Write the number on the line.

1. Circle the TALLEST.

2. **X** the SHORTEST.

3. How many cubes

   in the other tower? _____

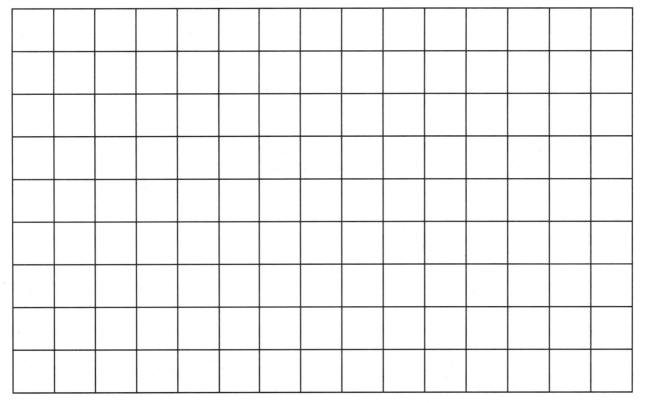

____   ____   ____

Puzzler

Color boxes to draw a picture.

What did you draw? _____

Reading & Math Practice, Grade 1 © 2014 Scholastic Inc.

FUN Phonics

Name each picture.
Write the missing letters.

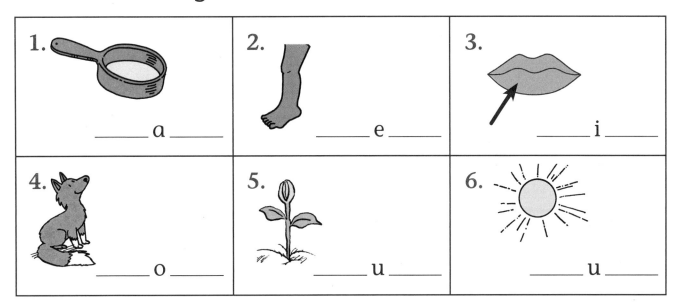

1. _____ a _____

2. _____ e _____

3. _____ i _____

4. _____ o _____

5. _____ u _____

6. _____ u _____

Handwriting Helper

✏ Trace. Then write.

get

give

glass

going

📖 Ready, Set, READ!

Read. Then answer the questions.

Riddle Time!

What key will never open a lock?

Answer: a tur-key!

What ant can break a table?

Answer: a gi-ant!

1. What **can** a turkey do?

   ○ A. flap   ○ B. draw

2. Giants can break tables because they are

   _____ .

🌀 BrainTeaser 🌀

Color the words.
Use the key.

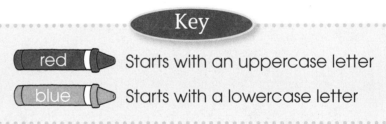

Key

red ▸ Starts with an uppercase letter

blue ▸ Starts with a lowercase letter

Big	can	You	not	See	kit
old	Dad	tub	Jet	him	May

Reading & Math Practice, Grade 1 © 2014 Scholastic Inc.

Number Place

Write how many.

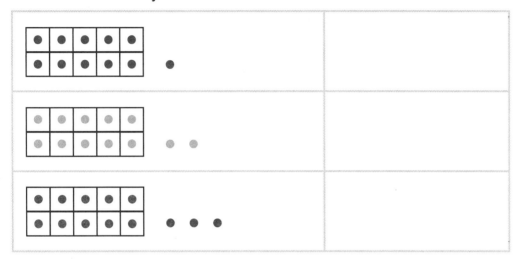

FAST Math

Circle all sums of 6.

6 + 1	3 + 3	1 + 5
2 + 4	4 + 3	4 + 2

Circle all sums of 7.

5 + 2	3 + 4	3 + 5
4 + 4	2 + 5	1 + 6

Think Tank

I am more than 10.
I am less than 18.
You say me when
you count by 5s.
What number am I?

Show your work
in the tank.

Data Place

How many? Make a table about you.

I have:

Number	Body Part
	Elbows
	Knees
	Mouth
	Thumbs
	Toes
More Than 10	
More Than 100	

Puzzler

Answer the questions about the picture.

How many dots **on** the L? _____

How many dots **inside** the L? _____

How many dots **outside** the L? _____

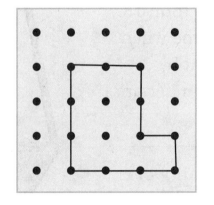

FUN Phonics

Name each picture.
Circle the letter that stands for the **middle** sound.

1.	2.	3.
h k m	g n w	c n b
4.	5.	6.
d l s	n s v	n p t

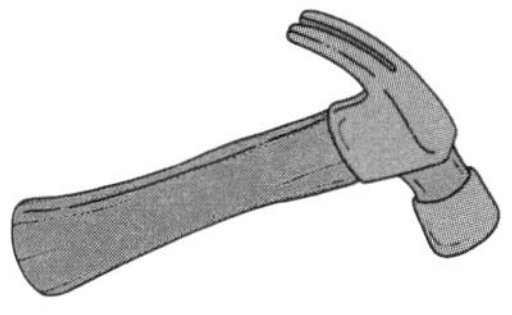

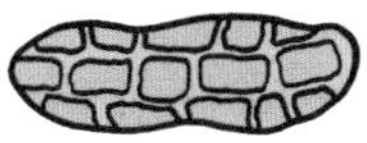

Handwriting Helper

✎ Trace. Then write.

him

her

have

help

📖 Ready, Set, READ!

Read.

Then answer the questions.

How They Go

The bee will fly.
The dog will run.
The pig will walk.
The frog will jump.
The duck will swim.

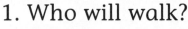

1. Who will walk?
   ○ A. the dog
   ○ B. the pig

2. How does the frog go?

   _____

   _____

🌀 BrainTeaser 🌀

Use the key to color the fish.

Key

| 1 red | 2 pink | 3 blue | 4 orange |
| 5 brown | 6 green | 7 purple | 8 yellow |

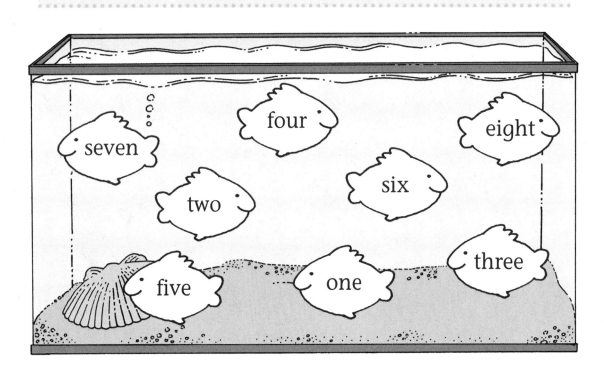

Number Place

Write how many.

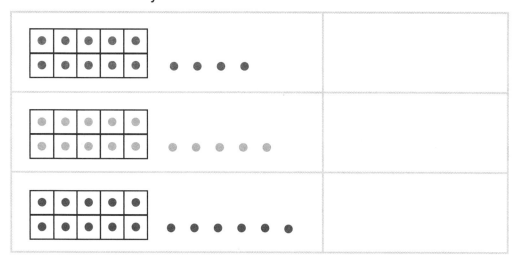

FAST Math

Circle all sums of 8.

6 + 2	3 + 4	1 + 7
4 + 4	5 + 3	7 + 2

Circle all sums of 9.

7 + 2	3 + 6	3 + 5
4 + 4	5 + 4	8 + 1

Think Tank

Blaze and Star are horses. They need shoes for each hoof. How many horseshoes do they need in all?

_____ horseshoes

Show your work in the tank.

Data Place

Use the graph to answer the questions.

Keys We Have

Rosa	🔑	🔑	🔑			
Kyle	🔑	🔑	🔑	🔑	🔑	🔑
Isaac	🔑	🔑	🔑	🔑		

1. How many children have keys? _____

2. Who has the most keys? _____

3. How many keys does Isaac have? _____

Puzzler

What bird has the biggest eyes?

Use the clues below to answer the question.

_____ _____ _____ _____ _____ _____ _____

The third letter is t.   The fourth letter is r.

The seventh letter is h.   The first letter is o.

The fifth letter is i.   The sixth letters is c.

The second letter is s.

Reading & Math Practice, Grade 1 © 2014 Scholastic Inc.

FUN Phonics

Circle the word that names each picture.

1. 	him ham hum	2. 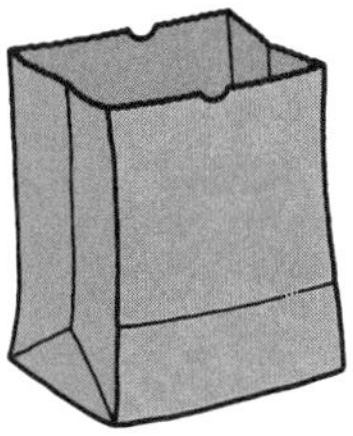	bug big bag	3. 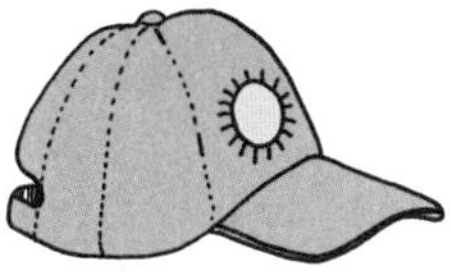	cap cop cup
4. 	gas glass grass	5. 	fun fin fan	6. 	pad pod bad

Handwriting Helper

✎ Trace. Then write.

just

just

joke

jump

📖 Ready, Set, READ!

Read. Then answer the questions.

What and Why

What is the longest word of all?
Answer: **Smiles**

Why is it so long?
Answer: It has a **mile** between
the first and last letters!

1. What kind of riddle is this?
   ○ A. math riddle   ○ B. word riddle

2. Is **smiles** <u>really</u> a long word? _____

🌀 BrainTeaser 🌀

Read the words in the word bank.
Sort and write them in the chart.

Word Bank

| arm | Gus | hill |
| hip | Nan | sea |

Names	Places	Body Words

Reading & Math Practice, Grade 1 © 2014 Scholastic Inc.

Number Place

Write how many.

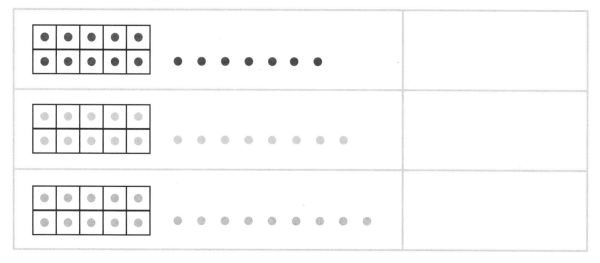

FAST Math

Write each missing addend.

$$\begin{array}{c} \boxed{} \\ +\ 4 \\ \hline 1\,0 \end{array} \qquad \begin{array}{c} \boxed{} \\ +\ 7 \\ \hline 1\,0 \end{array} \qquad \begin{array}{c} \boxed{} \\ +\ 2 \\ \hline 1\,0 \end{array} \qquad \begin{array}{c} \boxed{} \\ +\ 3 \\ \hline 1\,0 \end{array} \qquad \begin{array}{c} \boxed{} \\ +\ 6 \\ \hline 1\,0 \end{array}$$

💡 Think Tank

Greg has 7 books. He did not read 1 of them. How many books did he read?

He read _____ books.

Show your work in the tank.

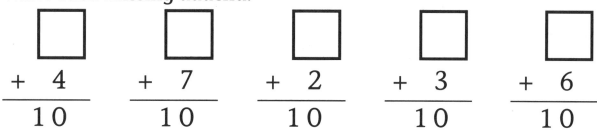

Think Tank

Data Place

Use the graph to answer the questions.

Seashells We Found

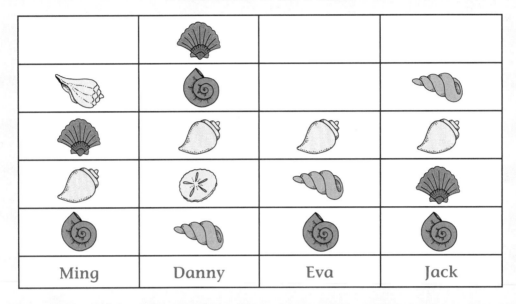

| Ming | Danny | Eva | Jack |

1. How many children found shells? _____

2. Who found the fewest shells? _____

3. Two children found 4 shells each. Write their names.

_____ and _____

Puzzler

Find each shape sum.
Use the numbers in the shapes.

② ③ 4

1. ⬦ = _____

2. ▭ = _____

3. ▢◯▢ = _____

4. Draw a shape sum for 7 below.

Reading & Math Practice, Grade 1 © 2014 Scholastic Inc.

FUN Phonics

Circle the word that names each picture.

1. 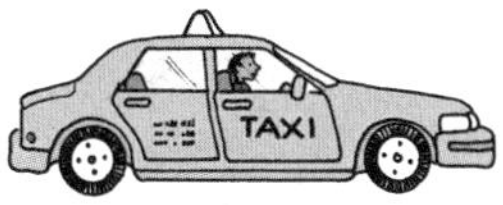 cab cob cub	2. 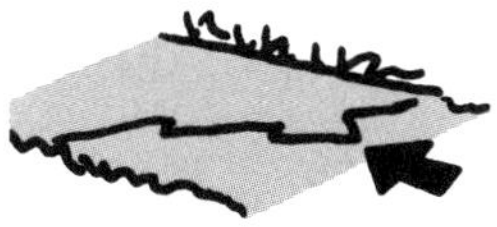 crock crook crack	3. 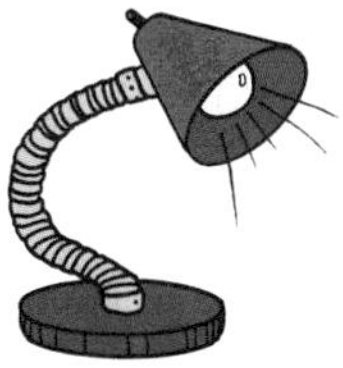 lump lamp limp
4. 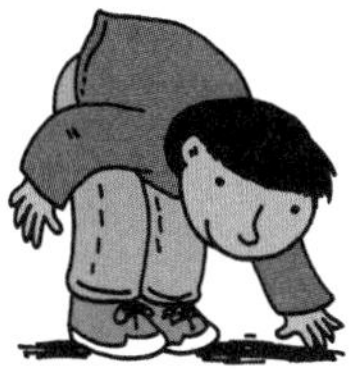 bend bang band	5. 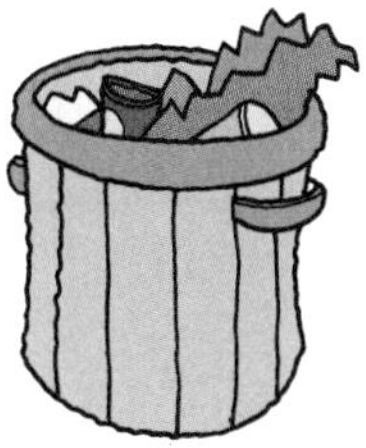 trash train troop	6. 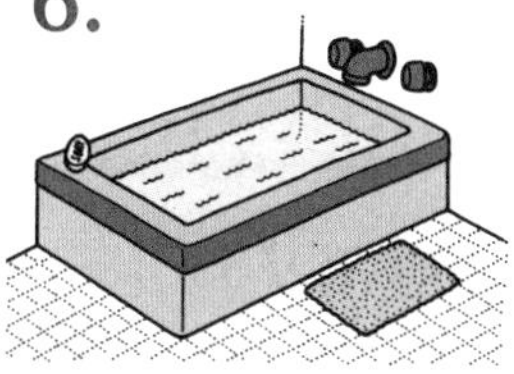 both Beth bath

Handwriting Helper

Trace. Then write.

left

like

looks

little

📖 Ready, Set, READ!

Read. Then answer the questions.

Two Jokes

Knock, knock!
 —Who's there?
Cargo.
 —Cargo who?
Car goes **zoom**!

Knock, knock!
 —Who's there?
Cows.
 —Cows who?
No, silly! Cows **moo**!

Moo!

1. Both jokes have to do with
   ○ A. doors.   ○ B. sounds.

2. How many questions are in each joke? _____

🌀 BrainTeaser 🌀

Read the words in the word bank.
Sort and write them in the chart.

Word Bank

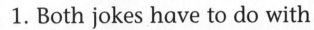

beef	fig	lamb
grapes	water	milk
plum	tea	ham

Fruits	Meats	Drinks

Reading & Math Practice, Grade 1 © 2014 Scholastic Inc.

Number Place

Draw lines to make matches.

1 ten 0 ones •	• 13
1 ten 1 one •	• 14
1 ten 2 ones •	• 11
1 ten 3 ones •	• 12
1 ten 4 ones •	• 10

1 ten 5 ones •	• 18
1 ten 6 ones •	• 15
1 ten 7 ones •	• 19
1 ten 8 ones •	• 16
1 ten 9 ones •	• 17

FAST Math

Subtract.

6 – 1 = _____   5 – 2 = _____   4 – 3 = _____

5 – 3 = _____   4 – 2 = _____   6 – 2 = _____

Think Tank

Kim is shorter than Rob.
Max is taller than Rob.
Max is taller than Kim.
Draw and label the
boys from tallest
to shortest.

**Show your work
in the tank.**

Reading & Math Practice, Grade 1 © 2014 Scholastic Inc.

Data Place

Use the calendar to answer the questions.

Bikes in the Bike Rack

Monday	Tuesday	Wednesday	Thursday	Friday
0	4	9	5	7

1. When were there no bikes in the rack? _____

2. How many bikes were in the rack on Friday? _____

3. Which day had 1 less bike than Thursday? _____

Puzzler

Roll a number cube. Write the number in a box.
Repeat to fill each **+** or **–** problem. Then solve.

1. ☐ + ☐ = ☐   4. ☐ – ☐ = ☐

2. ☐ + ☐ = ☐   5. ☐ – ☐ = ☐

3. ☐ + ☐ = ☐   6. ☐ – ☐ = ☐

Reading & Math Practice, Grade 1 © 2014 Scholastic Inc.

FUN Phonics

Circle the word that names each picture.

1.  crab crib crop	**2.**  milk mike mush	**3.**  swing six swim
4.  ditch dash dish	**5.**  fast fist first	**6.**  hill hall hull

Handwriting Helper

✏ Trace. Then write.

milk

make

much

money

📖 Ready, Set, READ!

Read. Then answer the questions.

Dance Chant

Two hops this way.
Two hops that way.
This way, that way,
this way, that!

Now spin this way.
Now spin that way.
This way, that way,
spin and stop!

1. What do you do last?
   ○ A. hop   ○ B. stop

2. How can the chant help you dance?

   _____

   _____

   _____

   _____

🌀 BrainTeaser 🌀

Read the words in the word bank.
Sort and write them by their word family.

Word Bank

lip	mat
hat	flat
dip	trip

cat

_____

_____

_____

ship

_____

_____

_____

Reading & Math Practice, Grade 1 © 2014 Scholastic Inc.

Number Place

Finish the pattern.

3 tens =	30	7 tens =	
4 tens =		8 tens =	
5 tens =		9 tens =	
6 tens =		10 tens =	

FAST Math

Subtract.

9 – 7 = _____   8 – 2 = _____   7 – 3 = _____

8 – 5 = _____   7 – 4 = _____   9 – 6 = _____

Think Tank

Zina buys an ice pop for 1 dollar. She buys a puppet for 3 dollars. How much money does she spend?

_____ dollars

Show your work in the tank.

Data Place

Count each kind of animal.
Show how many in the graph.
Color 1 box for each animal.

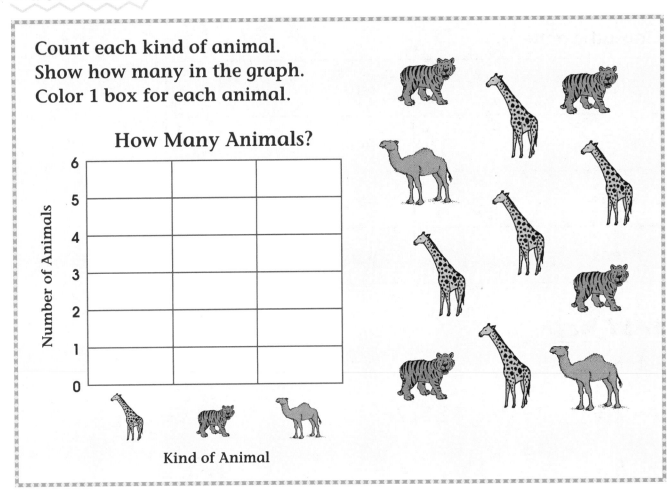

How Many Animals?

Number of Animals

Kind of Animal

Puzzler

Use number sense to solve each riddle.
Each picture stands for a number from 1 to 4.

If + = 2, then = _____

If + = 4, then = _____

If + = 8, then = _____

If + = 6, then = _____

FUN Phonics

Circle the word that names each picture.

1. 	lack lick lock	**2.** 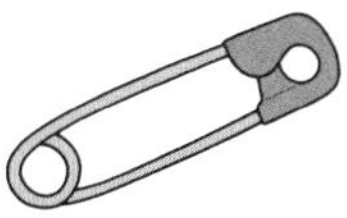	big bin pin	**3.** 	king kiss kilt
4. 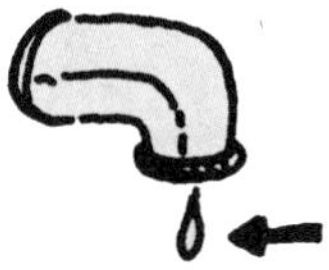	drift drip drink	**5.** 	nut net knit	**6.** 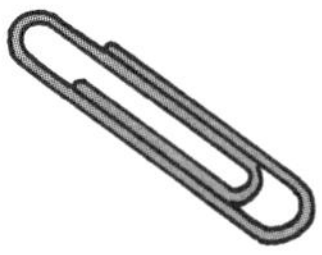	clip clap click

Handwriting Helper

✏ Trace. Then write.

now

neck

noon

night

📖 Ready, Set, READ!

Read. Then answer the questions.

A Wish

Now and then I wish that I
could be a kite up in the sky.
I'd ride upon the wind and go
any way the **breezes** blow.

1. Another word
   for **breezes** is
   ○ A. winds.
   ○ B. storms.

2. What is fun about
   being a kite?

   _____

   _____

   _____

🌀 BrainTeaser 🌀

Read the words in the word bank.
Sort and write them by their word family.

Word Bank

tail	twig
wig	Gail
mail	big

snail

_____

_____

_____

pig

_____

_____

_____

Number Place

Finish each number.

26 = __2__ tens 6 ones	54 = 5 tens _____ ones
47 = _____ tens 7 ones	82 = 8 tens _____ ones
39 = _____ tens 9 ones	75 = 7 tens _____ ones

FAST Math

Subtract. Think about doubles.

10 – 5 = _____   8 – 4 = _____   6 – 3 = _____

6 – _____ = 3   10 – _____ = 5   4 – _____ = 2

Think Tank

Libby has a nickel. Then she finds 2 copper coins. Now how much money does Libby have?

_____ cents

Show your work in the tank.

Data Place

Use the graph to answer the questions.

Our Hats

Becky								
Randy								
Freddy								

1. How many hats does Freddy have? _____

2. Who has 5 hats? _____

3. How many hats do Randy AND Becky have? _____

Puzzler

Letters have different shapes.

Straight Lines

A AND **T**

Curves

C AND **S**

Lines AND Curves

B AND **R**

Sort these letters: D E G H J K O P Q U V Z

Lines Only	Curves Only	Lines AND Curves

FUN Phonics

Circle the word that names each picture.

1. 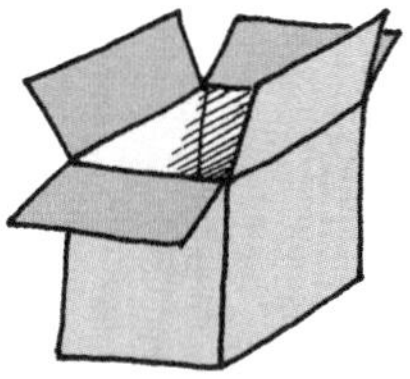 backs bucks box	2. 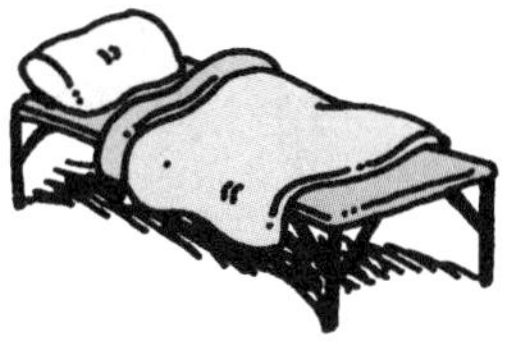 clot cat cot	3.  mop mod map
4. 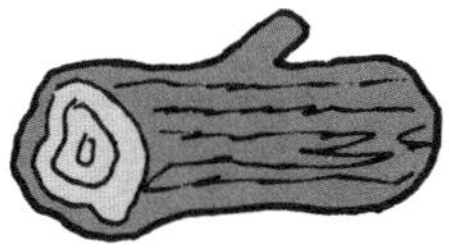 lot let log	5.  sack sock sick	6.  pond sand pump

Handwriting Helper

✎ Trace. Then write.

one

out

over

older

📖 Ready, Set, READ!

Read. Then answer the questions.

Moon Facts?

1. A cow jumped over the moon.
2. The moon has mountains on it.
3. Cows live on the moon.
4. People have walked on the moon.
5. The moon is made of green cheese.

1. What animal jumped over the moon?
   - ○ A. cow
   - ○ B. mouse

2. Which moon facts are **not** true? Write the numbers.

_____

🌀 BrainTeaser 🌀

Read the words in the word bank.
Sort and write them by their word family.

Word Bank

spot	dot
spell	well
tell	not

bell

_____

_____

_____

pot

_____

_____

_____

Number Place

Write the number.

6 tens 3 ones = 63	
5 tens 8 ones =	
9 tens 4 ones =	

7 tens 1 one =	
4 tens 9 ones =	
2 tens 6 ones =	

FAST Math

Add or subtract.

$$\begin{array}{r} 4 \\ + 5 \\ \hline \end{array} \qquad \begin{array}{r} 8 \\ - 5 \\ \hline \end{array} \qquad \begin{array}{r} 3 \\ + 6 \\ \hline \end{array} \qquad \begin{array}{r} 9 \\ - 4 \\ \hline \end{array} \qquad \begin{array}{r} 7 \\ - 6 \\ \hline \end{array}$$

Think Tank

Draw a shape that has 3 sides. Make 2 sides the same length. Write the name of the shape.

_____

Show your work in the tank.

Data Place

Use the chart to answer the questions.

Toy		How much?
Bell 		5¢
Frisbee 		10¢
Ball 		7¢
Yo-Yo 		3¢

1. You buy 2 bells. How much do you spend? _____

2. Which 2 different toys cost the same as a Frisbee? _____

   and _____

3. You spend 8¢ on 2 toys. What do you buy? _____

Puzzler

Each row has a different pattern. Draw what comes next.

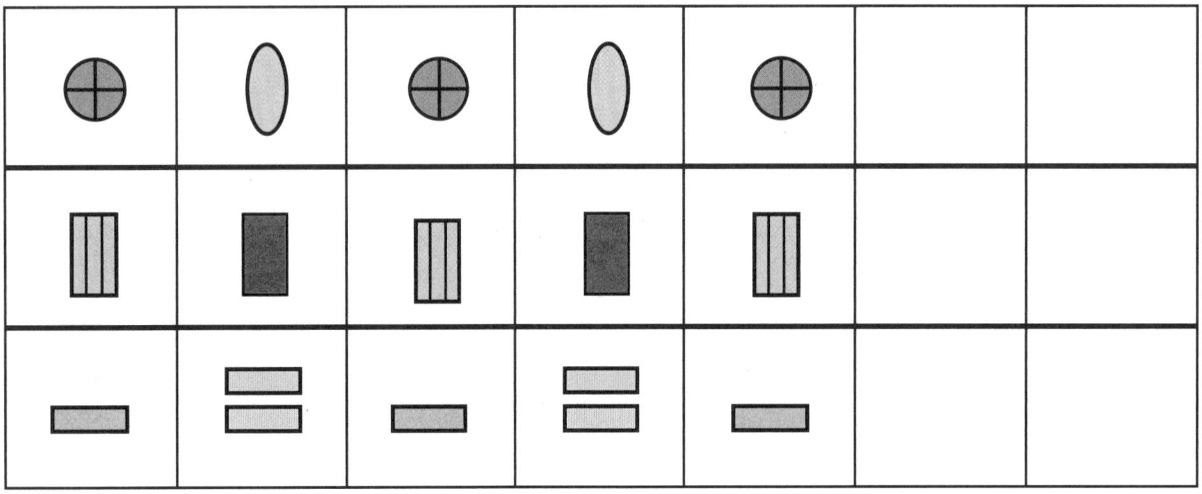

58

FUN Phonics

Circle the word that names each picture.

1. red / rid / rod	**2.** stop / slop / shop	**3.** lox / figs / fox
4. fog / frog / from	**5.** nab / nub / knob	**6.** clock / cluck / click

Handwriting Helper

✎ Trace. Then write.

push

play

picks

Denny

📖 Ready, Set, READ!

Read. Then answer the questions.

So Glad

Rain on the rooftop.
Rain on the tree.
Rain on the grass,
but not on me!

Dry in my raincoat.
Dry in my hat.
Dry in my boots.
Thanks for all that!

1. What kind
   of day is it?
   ○ A. wet
   ○ B. dry

2. Another word
   for **glad** is

   _____.

🌀 BrainTeaser 🌀

Read the words in the word bank.
Sort and write them by their word family.

Word Bank

wink	rock
pink	block
lock	drink

s<u>ink</u>

_____

_____

_____

s<u>ock</u>

_____

_____

_____

Number Place

Write each number.

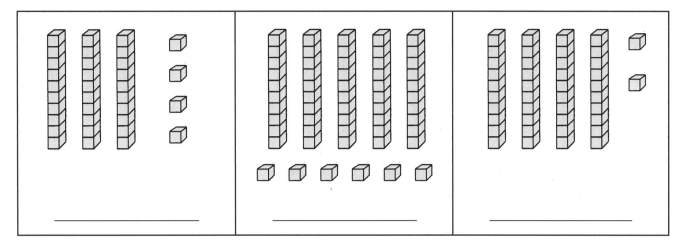

_____   _____   _____

FAST Math

Add.

4 + 9 = _____   5 + 7 = _____   8 + 3 = _____

6 + 8 = _____   7 + 6 = _____   3 + 9 = _____

Think Tank

Edgar has 8 stickers.
He gives some to Ana.
Then Edgar has 5 stickers.
How many did Ana get?

Ana got _____
stickers.

Show your work
in the tank.

Data Place

Twelve friends cut out pictures of the fruits they like best.

Use the grid to answer the questions.

1. How many friends cut out fruits? _____

2. How many different kinds of fruits did they pick? _____

3. Which fruit got picked the most? _____

Puzzler

Connect the dots in order. Start at 1.

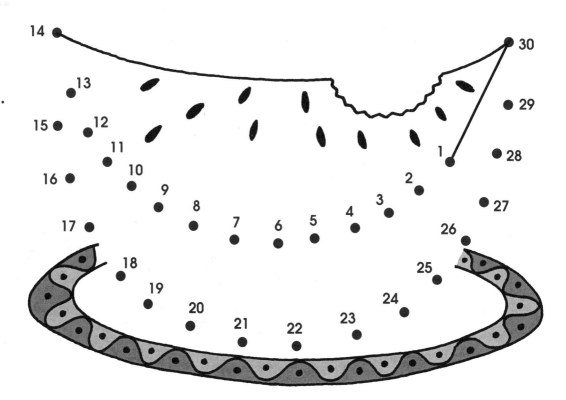

Reading & Math Practice, Grade 1 © 2014 Scholastic Inc.

FUN Phonics

Circle the word that names each picture.

1. tab tug tub	**2.** bud bed bad	**3.** mum mug rug
4. son sun spun	**5.** bass boss bus	**6.** hush hint hump

Handwriting Helper

✐ Trace. Then write.

rain

rest

rope

round

📖 Ready, Set, READ!

Read. Then answer the questions.

Standing Tall

How does a big lighthouse stay up?
Here are some facts.

- It is heavy and **sturdy**.
- Its parts fit together well.
- Some of it is under the ground.

1. Which other title best fits the text?
   ○ A. Made to Last   ○ B. Not Safe

2. What does **sturdy** mean?

_____

🌀 BrainTeaser 🌀

Write three more words for each word family.

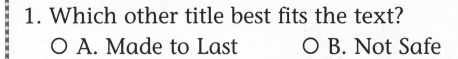

r<u>a</u>m

_____

_____

_____

to<u>p</u>

_____

_____

_____

Reading & Math Practice, Grade 1 © 2014 Scholastic Inc.

Number Place

Write the number.

Tens	Ones
9	1

Tens	Ones
7	3

Tens	Ones
6	8

_____   _____   _____

FAST Math

Add.

7 + 9 = _____   9 + 8 = _____   8 + 7 = _____

6 + 9 = _____   8 + 8 = _____   9 + 9 = _____

Think Tank

Van has 10¢.
He buys a pin for 6¢.
How much money
does he still have?
Van still has

_____ ¢.

Show your work
in the tank.

Data Place

Count and graph the shapes. Color 1 box for each shape.

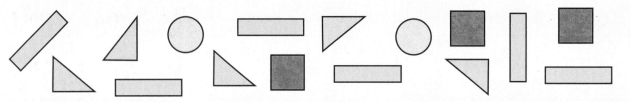

Different Shapes

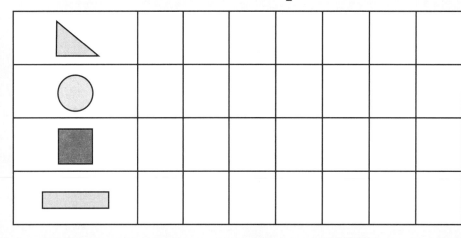

Number of Shapes

1. How many circles? _____

2. How many more triangles than squares? _____

3. How many shapes in all? _____

Puzzler

X the number in each set that does not belong.

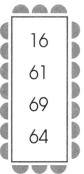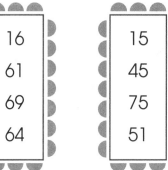

40	77	16	15	27
56	55	61	45	19
30	33	69	75	36
70	12	64	51	45

Reading & Math Practice, Grade 1 © 2014 Scholastic Inc.

FUN Phonics

Circle the word that names each picture.

1.  blush brush bush	2.  dust dish dent	3.  pug pump plug
4. 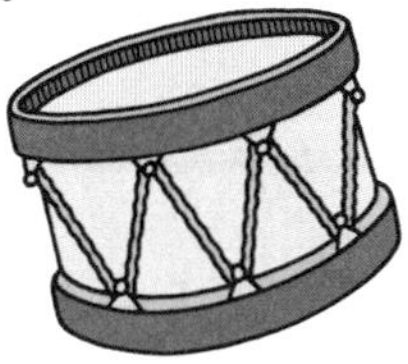 dim dime drum	5.  track trick truck	6.  skull skunk sunk

Handwriting Helper

✎ Trace. Then write.

said

slow

spoon

snake

📖 Ready, Set, READ!

Read. Then answer the questions.

Wake Up

Now the night is done.
Time to greet the sun.
Wake up, sleepyhead!
Jump up out of bed.
Make your bed look **neat**.
Have some eggs to eat.

1. When does the poem take place?
   ○ A. night   ○ B. morning

2. What does **neat** mean?

_____

꩜ BrainTeaser ꩜

Write three more words for each word family.

n<u>ee</u>d

_____

_____

_____

best

_____

_____

_____

Reading & Math Practice, Grade 1 © 2014 Scholastic Inc.

Number Place

Write how many tens and ones.

53 = _____ tens _____ ones   70 = _____ tens _____ ones

68 = _____ tens _____ ones   25 = _____ tens _____ ones

49 = _____ tens _____ ones   31 = _____ tens _____ ones

FAST Math

Add doubles.

```
   6          9          7          8          5
+  6       +  9       +  7       +  8       +  5
_____    _____     _____     _____     _____
```

Think Tank

A garden snake is 11 inches long. A milk snake is 4 inches shorter. Draw the snakes. How long is the milk snake?

_____ inches

Show your work in the tank.

Reading & Math Practice, Grade 1 © 2014 Scholastic Inc.

Data Place

Tally the pennies, nickels, and dimes.

How Many?

Coin	Tallies
 (penny)	
(nickel)	
(dime)	

Tally Marks			
1	I	6	⊞ I
2	II	7	⊞ II
3	III	8	⊞ III
4	IIII	9	⊞ IIII
5	⊞	10	⊞ ⊞

How many coins in all?

_____

Puzzler

Color the shapes. Use the key.

Key	
Shape	**Color**
☐	yellow
○	orange
△	red
▭	blue

70

Reading & Math Practice, Grade 1 © 2014 Scholastic Inc.

FUN Phonics

Circle the word that names each picture.

1.  hang hunt hen	2. 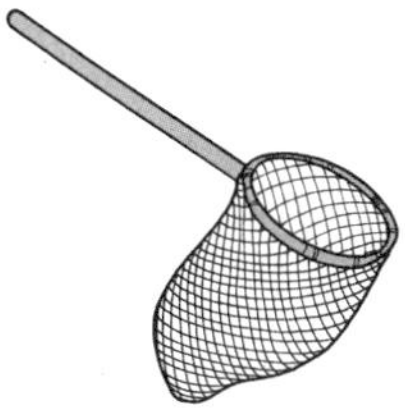 nut net knit	3.  ten tint tent
4.  sled slid slop	5.  vast vest vent	6.  stop slap step

Handwriting Helper

✎ Trace. Then write.

two

truck

thing

three

📖 Ready, Set, READ!

Read. Then answer the questions.

Your Brain

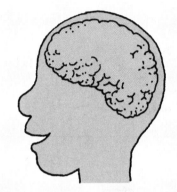

The brain is a part of your body.
It is inside your head. It is safe there.
The brain runs your body. It is like
your very own control center. It lets
you see, hear, smell, taste, and feel.
It lets you talk, think, and dream.
The brain is the boss!

1. The brain is so important because it
   ○ A. runs your body.   ○ B. is on the top.

2. Why do you think your head is hard?

_____

⊚ BrainTeaser ⊚

Fill in the missing word.
Each answer rhymes.

1. sack for old cloths   **rag** _____

2. skinny fish part   **thin** _____

3. baby bird with the flu   _____ **chick**

72

Reading & Math Practice, Grade 1 © 2014 Scholastic Inc.

Number Place

Write the missing numbers.

1		3		5		7		9	
11		13		15		17		19	
21		23		25		27		29	
31		33		35		37		39	

FAST Math ▶

Add.

$7 + 3 + 6 =$ _____ $2 + 5 + 8 =$ _____

$5 + 9 + 4 =$ _____ $7 + 6 + 5 =$ _____

💡 Think Tank

Carly found 11 nests.
Rob found 8 nests.
Who found fewer?

_____

How many fewer?

_____

Show your work
in the tank.

Data Place

Clark collects clocks.
Some have numbers AND hands.
Some have numbers ONLY.

Count and tally each kind.

How Many?

Clocks with:	Tallies
Numbers AND Hands	
Numbers ONLY	

How many more clocks have

numbers ONLY? _____

Puzzler

Look for sums of 10.
Use only 2 boxes for each sum.
Circle every sum you find.
One is done for you.

Hints:

• Find 6 more sums that go
  up and down ↕.

• Find 6 sums that go across ←→.

3	4	8	2	1
7	6	2	4	9
2	5	5	7	3
8	1	9	2	6
1	9	3	7	4

FUN Phonics

Circle the word that names each picture.

1.	bolt	2.	shall	3.	check
	built		shell		cheek
	belt		shale		chick
4.	bunch	5.	disk	6.	bend
	band		desk		break
	bench		dusk		bread

Handwriting Helper

✎ Trace. Then write.

untie

uncle

under

upon

Ready, Set, READ!

Read. Then answer the questions.

Let's Bake

Jen bakes cakes.
She bakes white cakes and pink cakes.
Tim bakes pies.
He bakes apple pies and lemon pies.
Sue bakes bread.
She bakes corn bread and white bread.
Which ones do you like to eat?

1. Finish the sentence.
   Tim bakes
   ○ A. bread   ○ B. pies

2. Who bakes cakes?
   ○ A. Jen   ○ B. Sue

☺ BrainTeaser ☺

Write two more words whose letters fit this shape.

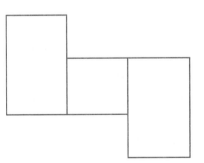
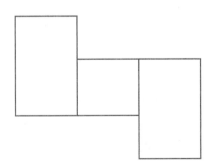

Reading & Math Practice, Grade 1 © 2014 Scholastic Inc.

Number Place

Count ON from each number.

36			

48			

29			

57			

FAST Math

Subtract.

$$\begin{array}{r} 14 \\ -\ 5 \\ \hline \end{array} \qquad \begin{array}{r} 13 \\ -\ 8 \\ \hline \end{array} \qquad \begin{array}{r} 11 \\ -\ 6 \\ \hline \end{array} \qquad \begin{array}{r} 12 \\ -\ 4 \\ \hline \end{array} \qquad \begin{array}{r} 13 \\ -\ 7 \\ \hline \end{array}$$

Think Tank

Kay is 9 years old. Finn is 4 years younger than Kay. Dirk is 2 years older than Finn. How old is Dirk?

_____ years old

Show your work in the tank.

Data Place

Use the table to answer the questions.

Pet Food Sold on Monday

Pet	🐦	🐱	🐶	🐟
Bags Sold	5	17	20	7

1. How many bags of bird food were sold? _____

2. Which pet owners got 20 bags of food? _____

3. How much more cat food sold than fish food? _____

Puzzler

Trace the shapes. Use the key.

Key	
Shape	**Color**
⬭	orange
△	green
○	yellow
□	brown
▭	blue
⬡	red

FUN Phonics

Circle the word that names each picture.

1.	rock	2.	tap	3.	vase
	rook		tape		vise
	rake		type		ways
4.	wave	5.	spade	6.	skate
	whale		shave		scoot
	wail		shade		skit

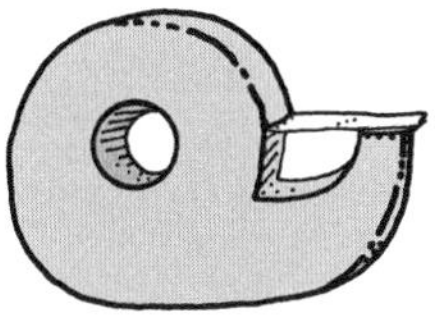

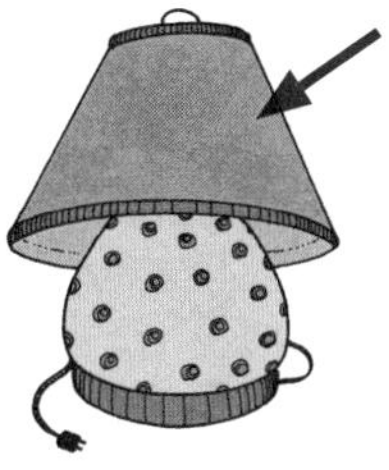

Handwriting Helper

✎ Trace. Then write.

want

walk

west

where

📖 Ready, Set, READ!

Read. Then answer the questions.

Where Is . . .

Where is my hair?   On my head!

Where is my neck?   Under my head!

Where are my teeth? In my mouth!

Where are my toes?   On my feet!

Where is my skin?   All over me!

1. What is in your mouth?
   - ○ A. hair
   - ○ B. teeth

2. Which is near your neck?
   - ○ A. your shoulders
   - ○ B. your elbows

🌀 BrainTeaser 🌀

Write two more words whose letters fit this shape.

fish

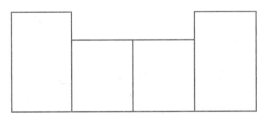

Number Place

Count BACK from each number.

			99

			87

			73

			61

FAST Math

Subtract.

$$18 - 9$$ $$15 - 8$$ $$17 - 9$$ $$16 - 7$$ $$15 - 7$$

____   ____   ____   ____   ____

Think Tank

Draw the next 3 in each pattern.

□ ● □ ● □ ● □ ____ ____ ____

E = A + E = A + ____ ____ ____

⓪ ① ⓪ ② ⓪ ③ ⓪ ____ ____ ____

Data Place

Use the Venn diagram to answer the questions.

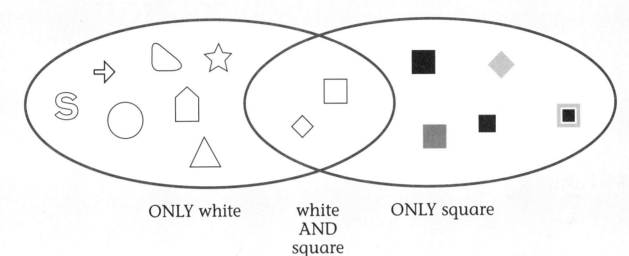

ONLY white   white AND square   ONLY square

Count the shapes in the diagram. How many are:

1. ONLY white? _____

2. ONLY square? _____

3. white AND square? _____

Puzzler

Most numbers on a phone match letters.
Find the value of each word.
Add the numbers to get the sum.

EXAMPLE
HAY $4 + 2 + 9 = 15$

FOX _____

WIN _____

LAW _____

VET _____

BUG _____

Reading & Math Practice, Grade 1 © 2014 Scholastic Inc.

FUN Phonics

Circle the word that names each picture.

1. sell sill sail	2. plain plate place	3. snail stale sail
4. try tray tree	5. pint paint paid	6. tune treat train

Handwriting Helper

✏️ Trace. Then write.

Andy

Bart

Clay

David

Ready, Set, READ!

Read. Then answer the questions.

Moles, Voles, or Both?

Moles AND Voles
Both have fur.
Both dig a lot.
Both hurt gardens.

ONLY Moles
eat insects.
have big paws.
have long noses.

ONLY Voles
eat plants.
have small paws.
have short noses.

1. What can both animals hurt? _____

2. Which animals eat plants? _____

3. Which animals have big paws? _____

BrainTeaser

Write one vowel to spell **two** words.

	t	
l	g	
	p	

	b	
w		n
	t	

	m	
c		p
	g	

Reading & Math Practice, Grade 1 © 2014 Scholastic Inc.

Number Place

Count. Circle groups of 10. Write how many.

❀ ❀	☼ ☼
_____ tens _____ ones	_____ tens _____ ones

FAST Math

Subtract. Think about doubles.

$14 - 7 =$ _____ $18 - 9 =$ _____ $12 - 6 =$ _____

$20 -$ _____ $= 10$ $16 -$ _____ $= 8$ $10 -$ _____ $= 5$

Think Tank

Jalal collects magnets. He has 8 magnets of animals. He has 9 magnets of boats. How many magnets does Jalal have? He has

_____ magnets.

Show your work in the tank.

Reading & Math Practice, Grade 1 © 2014 Scholastic Inc.

Data Place

Use the grid to answer the questions.

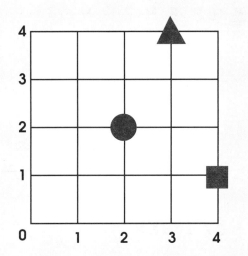

1. To find ●, start at 0.

   Go **across** _____ and then **up** _____ .

2. To find ▲, start at 0.

   Go **across** _____ and then **up** _____ .

3. To find ■, start at 0.

   Go **across** _____ and then **up** _____ .

4. Go **across** 1 and then **up** 3.

   Draw an **X**.

Puzzler

Figure out each pattern.
Write what comes next.

(1)(2)(1)(3)(1)(4)(   )(   )(   )

(4)(14)(24)(34)(44)(54)(   )(   )(   )

(3)(6)(9)(12)(15)(18)(21)(   )(   )(   )

(10)(5)(15)(10)(20)(15)(25)(   )(   )(   )

Reading & Math Practice, Grade 1 © 2014 Scholastic Inc.

FUN Phonics

Circle the word that names each picture.

1. 	noon neat nine	2. 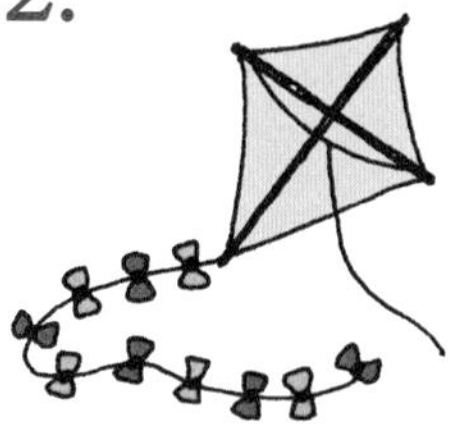	kit kite cut	3. 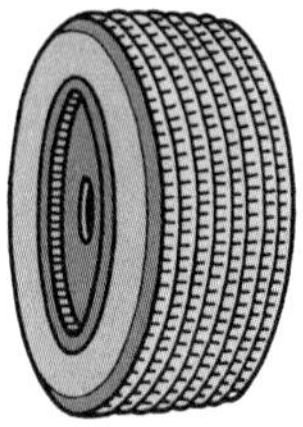	tire tear tore
4. 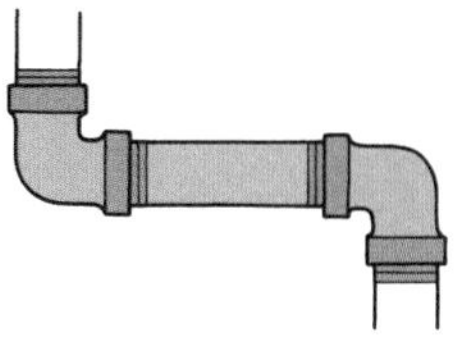	peep pipe pool	5. 	hook heck hike	6. 	dime dice dome

Handwriting Helper

✎ Trace. Then write.

Emma

Fiona

Owen

Hallie

📖 Ready, Set, READ!

Read. Then answer the questions.

Fact or Fiction?

Max the cat took a boat ride on the sea. A big wave tipped the boat over. Max fell out. He could not swim.

He was scared. A mermaid saved Max. She took Max to her sea cave. She showed Max her pet starfish.

1. Max could not
   ○ A. swim.
   ○ B. ride.

2. Who saved Max?
   ○ A. a boat
   ○ B. a mermaid

2. What tells you that the story is NOT true?

_____

🌀 BrainTeaser 🌀

What does each sign mean?
Draw lines to match the signs and words.

Trains cross here.   No dogs.   Don't go.

Reading & Math Practice, Grade 1 © 2014 Scholastic Inc.

Number Place

X the one in each row that does NOT belong.

33	3 tens 3 ones	3 + 3	thirty-three
65	6 tens 5 ones	60 + 5	sixty-four
87	9 tens 7 ones	90 + 7	ninety-seven
42	2 tens 4 ones	40 + 2	forty-two

FAST Math

Add or subtract.

$$\begin{array}{r} 15 \\ -\ 9 \\ \hline \end{array} \qquad \begin{array}{r} 9 \\ +\ 8 \\ \hline \end{array} \qquad \begin{array}{r} 11 \\ -\ 4 \\ \hline \end{array} \qquad \begin{array}{r} 8 \\ +\ 6 \\ \hline \end{array} \qquad \begin{array}{r} 16 \\ -\ 7 \\ \hline \end{array} \qquad \begin{array}{r} 7 \\ +\ 9 \\ \hline \end{array}$$

Think Tank

A magic show starts at 1:00. It lasts for 2 hours. What time is it when the show ends?

_____

In the tank, draw a clock to show the time.

Data Place

Use the graph to answer the questions.

Best Things to Collect

Cards	☺ ☺ ☺
Rocks	☺ ☺ ☺ ☺ ☺ ☺
Shells	☺ ☺ ☺ ☺ ☺ ☺ ☺ ☺

Key: ☺ = 1 vote

1. How many people voted for rocks? _____

2. How many people voted for cards? _____

3. Which is the favorite thing to collect? _____

4. How many people picked it? _____

Puzzler

Measure length with the lizard.
Find something for each length.

How Long?	What Is It?
Less Than 1 Lizard	
About 2 Lizards	
About 4 Lizards	
About 6 Lizards	
More Than 7 Lizards	

Reading & Math Practice, Grade 1 © 2014 Scholastic Inc.

FUN Phonics

Circle the word that names each picture.

1.  vine have hive	2. 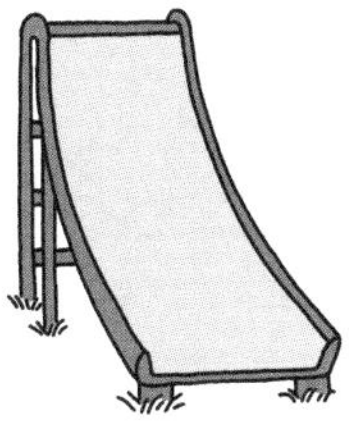 slid slide sleet	3. 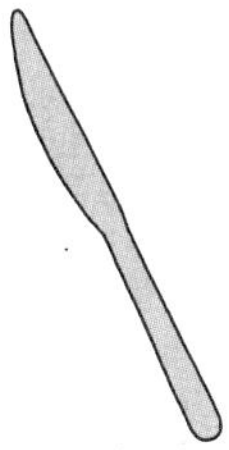 knife cuff fine
4.  mash mine mice	5.  smile smell small	6.  flee fly fry

Handwriting Helper

✐ Trace. Then write.

Inez

James

Kent

Lynn

📖 Ready, Set, READ!

Read. Then answer the questions.

Can It Jump?

Ask an egg to jump. It cannot.
Pick up an egg and put it down.
That is not a jump.
Roll the egg. It can roll.
But that is still not a jump.
AHA! An egg has no legs.
So an egg cannot jump.

1. Why can't an egg jump?

_____

2. AHA! means
   ○ A. Oh, no!   ○ B. Oh, I know!

🌀 BrainTeaser 🌀

Read and draw.

• a fish in the water
• a bird by the cloud
• a smile on the sun

Reading & Math Practice, Grade 1 © 2014 Scholastic Inc.

Number Place

Circle the value of the underlined digit.

5̲7		**45̲**		**6̲3**	
50	5	50	5	60	6
1̲8		**92̲**		**79̲**	
10	1	20	2	90	9

FAST Math

Write **+** or **−** in each cloud.

6 ☁ 3 = 9   12 ☁ 1 = 11   10 ☁ 3 = 7

8 ☁ 3 = 5   11 ☁ 2 = 13   9 ☁ 4 = 13

💡 Think Tank

Ondie buys ribbons.
She gets a red one for 15¢.
She gets a purple one
for 10¢. She gets a
silver one for 25¢.
How much does
Ondie spend in all?

_____ ¢

Show your work
in the tank.

Data Place

Use the graph to answer the questions.

Grandpa Goes Fishing

First Trip							
Second Trip							
Third Trip							

0　1　2　3　4　5　6　7

Number of Fish

1. How many times did Grandpa go fishing? _____

2. When did he catch the most fish? _____

3. When did he catch 5 fish? _____

Puzzler

Sort each number. Write it in the box where it belongs.
Then write your own number that can go in each box.

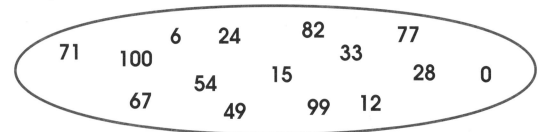

Numbers < 25	Numbers 26 to 70	Numbers > 70

Reading & Math Practice, Grade 1 © 2014 Scholastic Inc.

FUN Phonics

Circle the word that names each picture.

1.  come / cane / cone	**2.** 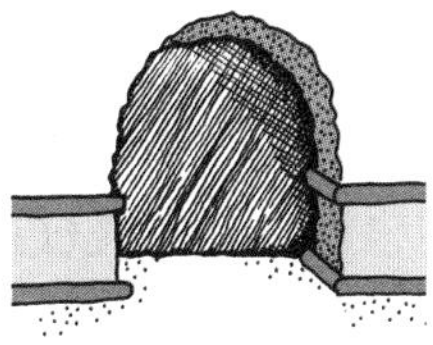 hope / hole / heel	**3.**  soak / smock / smoke
4. 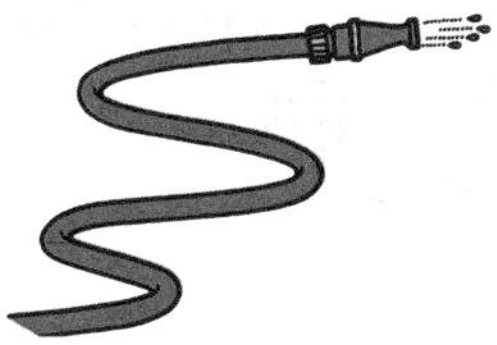 home / hose / house	**5.**  crow / cold / crown	**6.**  food / feed / fold

Handwriting Helper

✎ Trace. Then write.

Maria

Nell

Omar

Peter

📖 Ready, Set, READ!

Read. Then answer the questions.

The Band

"Let us make a band," says Bill.
"I can play drums," says Nan. Boom!
"I can play guitar," says Tom. Strum!
Inez plays a keyboard. She presses the white and black keys. Plink, plunk!
Bill hits a cowbell. Clang! "Now let us rock!" he says. And they all play.

1. Tom can play the
   ○ A. drums.   ○ B. guitar.   ○ C. keyboard.

2. How many kids play in the band? _____

🌀 BrainTeaser 🌀

Finish the man.
- Draw two eyes.
- Draw a ▲ nose.
- Draw a smile.
- Draw a beard.

96

Number Place

Write the number that comes just AFTER.

27, _____   48, _____   65, _____

36, _____   50, _____   79, _____

FAST Math

Solve.

If 5 + 7 = 12, then 12 − 5 = _____ .

If 13 − 5 = 8, then 8 + 5 = _____ .

If 9 + 8 = 17, then 17 − 9 = _____ .

If 16 − 7 = 9, then 7 + 9 = _____ .

Think Tank

The teacher serves fruit snacks. She gives bananas to 14 kids. She gives oranges to 9 kids. How many more kids snack on bananas than on oranges?

_____

Show your work in the tank.

Data Place

Use the graph to answer the questions.

At the Bake Sale

Number of Treats

Kind of Treat

1. How many kinds of treats were at the bake sale? _____

2. How many and sold?_____

3. Which 2 treats sold the same number? Circle them.

Puzzler

ESTIMATE means to make a smart guess.
Use ordinal numbers to name letters in the word ESTIMATE.

1. What is the fifth letter? _____

2. What is the second letter? _____

3. What is the fourth letter? _____

4. What is the sixth letter? _____

5. What letter is third and seventh?

   _____

6. ESTIMATE has 2 of the letter E.
   One E is the first letter. The other E
   is the _____ letter.

98

FUN Phonics

Circle the word that names each picture.

1. 	Steve stove stiff	2. 	globe gloom good	3. 	bow bowl blow
4. 	code coot coat	5. 	told toad tow	6. 	toast test toes

Handwriting Helper

✎ Trace. Then write.

Quinn

Rusty

Skye

Tate

Ready, Set, READ!

Read. Then answer the questions.

To Nell's House

1. Start at our school.
   Turn right onto Lark Way.

2. After three stop signs, turn left onto Bell Road. Drive about two miles.

3. After the car wash, turn right onto Gray Lane. Look for 53 Gray Lane. It is a red house on the left.

1. This is a set of
   ○ A. keys
   ○ B. directions

2. Where does Nell live?

   _____

   _____

   _____

   _____

꩜ BrainTeaser ꩜

Look at the pictures.
Find and circle the names for each in the puzzle.
Look across and down.

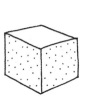

J	T	C	A	G	E	L	R
O	I	U	Q	U	A	K	O
S	R	B	N	E	S	T	S
J	E	E	P	M	R	O	E

Number Place

Write the number that comes just BEFORE.

_____ , 12   _____ , 45   _____ , 66

_____ , 31   _____ , 59   _____ , 80

FAST Math

Write the missing number.

$5 + $ _____ $= 12$ $11 - $ _____ $= 7$ $7 + $ _____ $= 15$

$6 + $ _____ $= 13$ $12 - $ _____ $= 9$ $13 - $ _____ $= 4$

Think Tank

Hakim buys an apple for 20¢. He also buys string cheese for 25¢. How much does he spend on his snack?

He spends _____ ¢.

Show your work in the tank.

Think Tank

Data Place

Write the number pair where you find each building or place.

One is done for you.

1. (1, 3)

2. _____

3. _____

4. _____

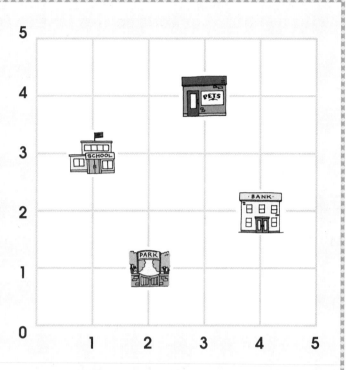

Puzzler

Color the shapes.
Use the key.

Key	
If the number is from	**Color the shape**
10 to 25	blue
26 to 40	red
41 to 55	yellow
56 to 70	purple
71 to 85	green
86 to 100	orange

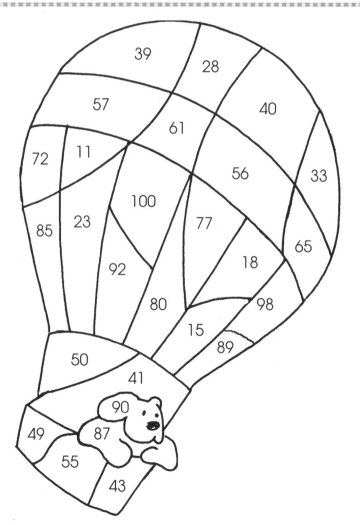

FUN Phonics

Circle the word that names each picture.

1. 	moo mile mule	2. 	flute fruit fret	3. 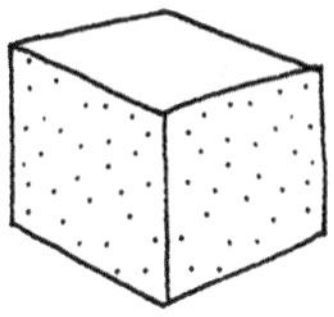	cube code cute
4. 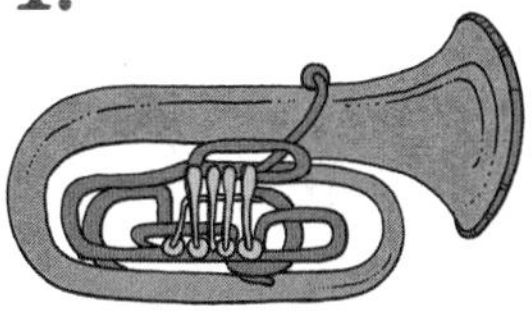	tube tuba tuna	5. 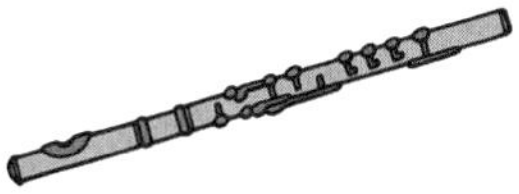	flood fleet flute	6. 	glue goo glee

Handwriting Helper

✎ Trace. Then write.

Tina

Val

Winn

Xavier

📖 Ready, Set, READ!

Read. Then answer the questions.

The New House

Today Glen saw his new house. It is not done yet. But he will move soon.

Glen saw his new room. It is big and sunny. It will have bunk beds. Glen hopes he gets to sleep on top.

Maybe moving will not be so bad.

1. What happened today?

_____

_____

_____

_____

2. How does Glen feel about moving?
   ○ A. excited
   ○ B. not sure

꩜ BrainTeaser ꩜

Look at the pictures.
Find and circle the names for each in the puzzle.
Look across and down.

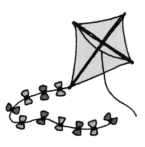

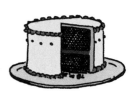

R	O	P	E	K	I	T	H
U	P	A	C	A	K	E	O
B	U	I	S	W	A	N	W
L	A	L	T	K	I	T	E

Number Place

Write the number that comes BEFORE and AFTER.

_____ , 17, _____   _____ , 75, _____

_____ , 31, _____   _____ , 60, _____

_____ , 96, _____   _____ , 42, _____

FAST Math

Count.
Write how much.
Circle the greater amount.

(coins)	_____ ¢
(coins)	_____ ¢

Think Tank

Nathan buys 3 hot dogs.
They cost $2 each.
How much does he
spend on hot dogs?

$ _____

Show your work
in the tank.

Data Place

Some numbers have lines ONLY.
Some have curves ONLY.
Some have lines AND curves.

| 0 1 2 3 4 5 6 7 8 9 |

Write 0 to 9 in the loops where they belong.

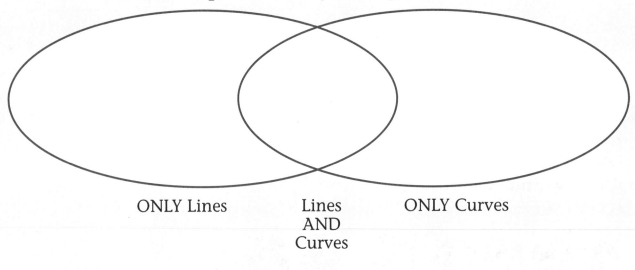

ONLY Lines   Lines AND Curves   ONLY Curves

Puzzler

**Three numbers in each balloon can make a number fact.
X the number that does NOT belong.**

Reading & Math Practice, Grade 1 © 2014 Scholastic Inc.

FUN Phonics

Circle the word that names each picture.

1. 	noon new knew	2. 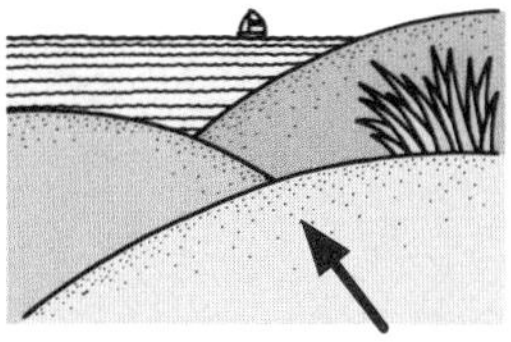	duke dune due	3. 	ruler rail reel
4. 	soot suit sweet	5. 	score scare screw	6. 	juice goose jewels

Handwriting Helper

✎ Trace. Then write.

Yoko

Zeka

What name do you like best?

📖 Ready, Set, READ!

Read. Then answer the questions.

Ships

A ship is a large boat.
It can sail a long way.
It can cross wide oceans.
It can go on deep rivers.
A **cargo** ship can carry giant loads.
A cargo ship can carry oil or pipes.
It can carry steel or cars.
Many things we use get here by ship.

1. What does **cargo** mean?

○ A. a large boat   ○ B. a giant load

2. Why don't cargo ships sail on ponds?

_____

🌀 BrainTeaser 🌀

Draw a line to match.

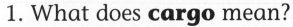

One	More Than One
bat •	• rings
hug •	• plates
ring •	• looks
look •	• hugs
plate •	• bats

Number Place

Write the missing numbers.

27, _____ , _____ , _____ , _____ , 32

48, _____ , _____ , _____ , _____ , 53

76, _____ , _____ , _____ , _____ , 81

FAST Math

Add or subtract. Write ¢.

10¢	7¢	9¢	15¢	16¢	9¢
− 2¢	+ 4¢	+ 3¢	− 5¢	− 8¢	+ 6¢
_____	_____	_____	_____	_____	_____

Think Tank

I am a 2-digit number.
I am less than 40.
I name all the fingers,
toes, eyes, and ears
you have.
What number am I?

_____

Show your work
in the tank.

Reading & Math Practice, Grade 1 © 2014 Scholastic Inc.

Data Place

The children in Ezra's class drew creepy crawlies. Then they counted their drawings.

Use the table to answer the questions.

Creepy Crawlies	
Slug	5
Snail	11
Worm	8

1. Which creepy crawly did 5 children draw? _____

2. How many snail pictures were there? _____

3. How many more worms than slugs? _____

Puzzler

Pretend that the thick line is a mirror.
Half of the design is ABOVE the mirror.
Shade the other half BELOW the thick line.

Reading & Math Practice, Grade 1 © 2014 Scholastic Inc.

FUN Phonics

Circle the word that names each picture.

1.  door deer dare	2.  shape sharp sheep	3.  seed said sand
4.  keen seen queen	5. 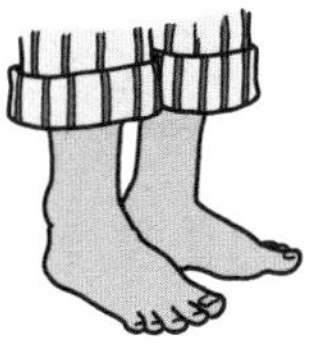 foot feet felt	6.  wheel where week

Handwriting Helper

✏️ Trace. Then write.

red

pink

green

yellow

📖 Ready, Set, READ!

Read. Then answer the questions.

A Noise

Li and Aya were walking home. They passed a tall tree.

The girls heard a spooky noise. Was it crying? They stopped walking. They held hands.

Then Aya smiled and pointed up. "Look!" she said.

Li saw the kitten. "Oh, kitty!" said Li. "We will get help for you."

1. Why did the girls hold hands?
   ○ A. to cross a street   ○ B. to feel safer

2. What made the noise?

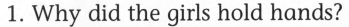

🌀 BrainTeaser 🌀

Finish the chart.

One	More Than One
house	houses
	rooms
	floors
	steps

Reading & Math Practice, Grade 1 © 2014 Scholastic Inc.

Number Place

Compare. Write **<** or **>**.

68 ◯ 62   74 ◯ 81   92 ◯ 90

45 ◯ 41   89 ◯ 93   52 ◯ 47

FAST Math

Solve. Draw lines to match facts in the same family.

6 + 7 = ☐ ●   ● 13 − 8 = ☐

9 + 8 = ☐ ●   ● 13 − 7 = ☐

8 + 5 = ☐ ●   ● 17 − 8 = ☐

Think Tank

Margo has 10 nickels.
She spends 3 of them
on gumballs. How many
nickels does Margo
still have? Margo has

_____ nickels.
It is the same as

_____ cents.

**Show your work
in the tank.**

Reading & Math Practice, Grade 1 © 2014 Scholastic Inc.

Data Place

Look at the boxes. Then draw each line. Start at ●.

Draw a line about 8 boxes long.

○ ●

Draw a line about 3 boxes long.

○ ●

Draw a line longer than 10 boxes.

○ ●

Order the lines from 1 (longest) to 3 (shortest).
Write the numbers in the circles.

Puzzler

Do a length hunt. Use your shoe as a "ruler."
Find 4 things for each part of the chart. List them.

Shorter than my shoe	About the Same as my shoe	Longer than my shoe

FUN Phonics

Circle the word that names each picture.

1.  tie toe tea	2. 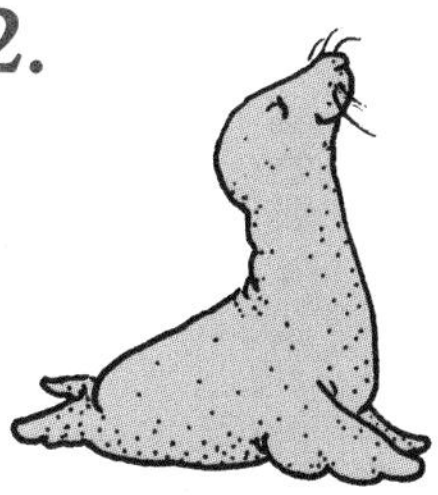 seal sell sill	3. 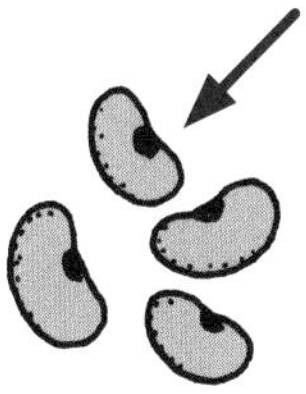 bone bean bun
4.  leach leaks leash	5.  bleak beak beat	6. 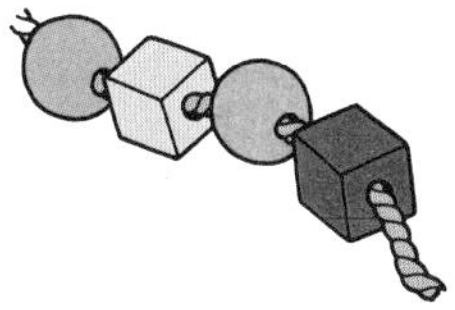 beds beads bends

Handwriting Helper

✎ Trace. Then write.

black

brown

purple

orange

📖 Ready, Set, READ!

Read. Then answer the questions.

Dear Hope,

   It is great at Gem Beach.
The ocean is so big! I swim
every day. I pick up shells.
I make sand castles. It is fun!

   Today I saw a bird dive for food.
It flew down fast. Then it came up
with a fish in its mouth.

   I miss you. See you soon.

Your Friend,
Dawn

1. Who wrote the postcard?
   ○ A. Hope   ○ B. Gem   ○ C. Dawn

2. Why did the bird dive?

_____

🌀 BrainTeaser 🌀

Finish each sentence.

1. Five peaches, but one _____ .

2. Two foxes, but one _____ .

3. Six kisses, but one _____ .

4. Four bushes, but one _____ .

Reading & Math Practice, Grade 1 © 2014 Scholastic Inc.

Number Place

Look at the numbers in the cloud.
Four are ODD. Four are EVEN.
Write the numbers in the chart.

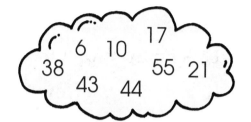

ODD Numbers	EVEN Numbers

FAST Math

Add.

$$\begin{array}{r} 36 \\ + \ 10 \\ \hline \end{array} \qquad \begin{array}{r} 83 \\ + \ 10 \\ \hline \end{array} \qquad \begin{array}{r} 57 \\ + \ 10 \\ \hline \end{array} \qquad \begin{array}{r} 64 \\ + \ 10 \\ \hline \end{array} \qquad \begin{array}{r} 75 \\ + \ 10 \\ \hline \end{array} \qquad \begin{array}{r} 49 \\ + \ 10 \\ \hline \end{array}$$

Think Tank

Grammy loves to bake.
She baked 6 cakes, 4 pies,
and 24 muffins. How
many things did she
bake in all? She baked

_____ things.

**Show your work
in the tank.**

Data Place

Color bars on the graph to show each price.

How Many Pennies?

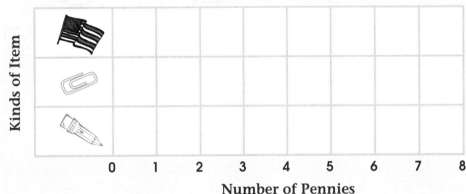

1. How much more for a 🏴 than a 📎 ? _____

2. How much for 6 📎 ? _____

3. How much for 1 of each item? _____

Puzzler

Each row has a different pattern.
Draw what comes next.

FUN Phonics

Write a rhyme for each word.
Use an *r* blend from the box.
Use each blend ONCE.

r Blends

br   cr   dr
fr   pr

seen	name	saw
green		

nice	back	loom

Handwriting Helper

✎ Trace. Then write.

now

later

after

before

📖 Ready, Set, READ!

Read. Then answer the questions.

Hungry

Ken rubs his tummy. He is hungry.
So he goes to the diner.
  "A hot dog, please," Ken says.
  "How do you like it?" asks the cook.
  "I like it just plain," says Ken.
  The cook makes Ken's hot dog.
Ken pays her. He eats his hot dog.
He rubs his tummy again. Now Ken is full.

1. Where did Ken go?
   ○ A. kitchen   ○ B. diner   ○ C. store

2. What do you like on your hot dog?

_____

🌀 BrainTeaser 🌀

Circle the **action** word.

1. A girl sleeps in her bed.

2. A jet flies in the sky.

Write an **action** word.

3. A snake _____ in the sand.

4. Jay _____ at the joke.

Reading & Math Practice, Grade 1 © 2014 Scholastic Inc.

Number Place

Skip count aloud by 5s. Write each number you say.

5, 10, _____ , _____ , _____ , _____ , _____ ,

40, _____ , _____ , _____ , _____ , _____ ,

_____ , 75, _____ , _____ , _____ , _____ , 100

FAST Math

Subtract.

45	98	56	61	73	84
- 10	- 10	- 10	- 10	- 10	- 10
_____	_____	_____	_____	_____	_____

Think Tank

Circle the shape in each row that does NOT belong.

Data Place

Mrs. Lobel took her class to lunch. She saw that 8 kids drank juice, 9 drank milk, and 6 kids drank water.

Show this data in a graph. Make bars with letters. Count from the bottom up.

- Write a **J** for each juice.

- Write an **M** for each milk.

- Write a **W** for each water.

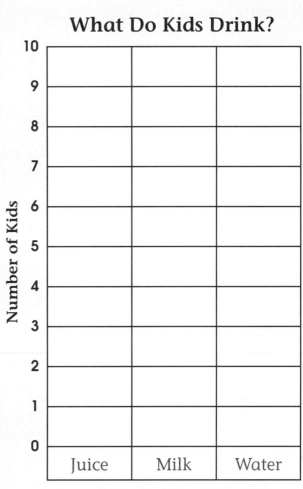

What Do Kids Drink?

Number of Kids — Kind of Drink

Juice | Milk | Water

Puzzler

Write 1, 3, 7, and 9 ONCE in each empty box. Make each row ↔ and column ↕ have a sum of 15.

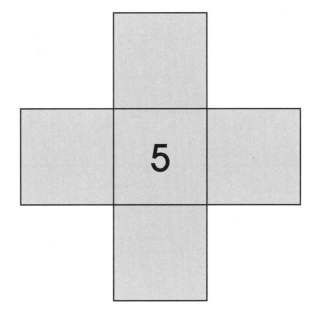

5

FUN Phonics

Write a rhyme for each word.
Use an *l* blend from the box.
Use each blend ONCE.

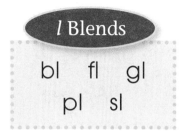

l Blends

bl fl gl
pl sl

mean	cane	deep
clean		

fast	robe	tag

Handwriting Helper

·······································

✎ Trace. Then write.

boy

girl

man

woman

📖 Ready, Set, READ!

Read. Then answer the questions.

Water

You need water every day to live. You get water in many foods you eat.

Apples and carrots have water in them. Milk is part water. Watermelon is full of water. The name tells you so.

Soup has lots of water in it. Ice is water, too. It melts when you suck it.

1. Why does it help to know foods that have water in them?

_____

2. Which food has more water in it?
   ○ A. peach   ○ B. cornflakes

🌀 BrainTeaser 🌀

Write each set of three words in ABC order.

shoe	jump	rib	much	flat	when

Number Place

Skip count aloud by 10s. Write each number you say.

10, _____ , _____ , _____ , _____ ,

_____ , _____ , _____ , _____ , 100

FAST Math

Add.

44	38	51	62	17	29
+ 30	+ 50	+ 40	+ 20	+ 60	+ 70

_____   _____   _____   _____   _____   _____

Think Tank

Each house on Key Road has a number. The first five house numbers are 101, 103, 105, 107, and 109. What is the next house number? The next

number is _____ .

Show your work in the tank.

Data Place

Kids told what they do before bed.

Use the data to make a graph.

Before bed I like to:	Tallies
Play with my pet.	⊕⊕⊕ |||
Read a book.	⊕⊕⊕ ⊕⊕⊕
Watch TV.	⊕⊕⊕	

What Kids Do Before Bed

Play with my pet.												
Read a book.												
Watch TV.												

0　　2　　4　　6　　8　　10　　12

Number of Votes

1. How many more kids read than watch TV? _____

2. How many kids play with a pet or watch TV? _____

Puzzler

Write how much each shape costs.

 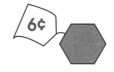

1.

 _____

2.

 _____

3.

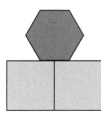 _____

4.

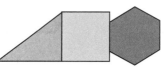 _____

Reading & Math Practice, Grade 1 © 2014 Scholastic Inc.

FUN Phonics

Write a rhyme for each word.
Use an *s* blend from the box.
Use each blend ONCE.

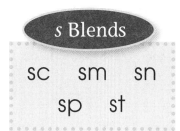

s Blends

sc   sm   sn
sp   st

dirt	rug	dream
skirt		

lace	tile	toot

Handwriting Helper

✎ Trace. Then write.

sister

brother

father

mother

📖 Ready, Set, READ!

Read. Then answer the questions.

Jobs

Bea is a farmer. She works all day. She grows beans. She works hard.

John is a painter. He works every day. He paints pictures. He loves colors.

Lulu is a cook. She works on weekends. She cooks soups. She loves food.

Ron is a dancer. He works at night. Ron teaches people to dance. He loves to dance.

1. Who works at night?
   ○ A. Lulu   ○ B. John   ○ C. Ron

2. Why do you think Lulu is a cook?

_____

🌀 BrainTeaser 🌀

Write each set of three words in ABC order.

run	start	line	horse	ride	boot

Reading & Math Practice, Grade 1 © 2014 Scholastic Inc.

Number Place

Count BACK aloud by 10s. Write the numbers you say.

100, 90, _____ , _____ , _____ , _____ ,

_____ , _____ , _____ , _____ , 0

FAST Math

Subtract.

85	92	51	64	78	39
− 60	− 70	− 40	− 30	− 50	− 20
_____	_____	_____	_____	_____	_____

Think Tank

The art teacher gets 32 new paintbrushes and 45 new markers. How many new art items is this in all?

_____ new
art items

Show your work in the tank.

Data Place

Darla cleaned her room. Look what she found under her bed!

Show the data in a graph. Color 1 box for each item.

Item	Tally
Crayons	卌 I
Socks	III
Toys	卌

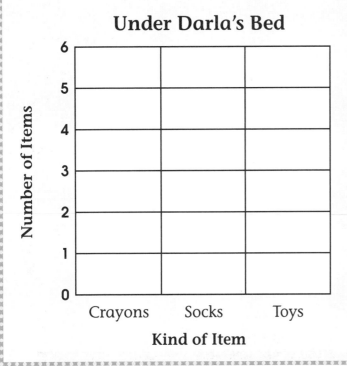

Under Darla's Bed

Number of Items

6
5
4
3
2
1
0

Crayons   Socks   Toys

Kind of Item

How many items did Darla find in all?

_____

Puzzler

**Draw the shapes.
Start and stop each line at a dot.**

Triangle

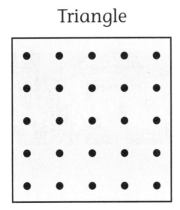

Square

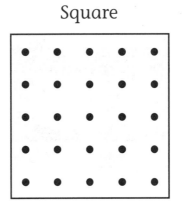

Rectangle

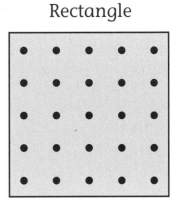

130

FUN Phonics

Circle the word that names each picture. Write its <u>final</u> <u>blend</u>.

1. 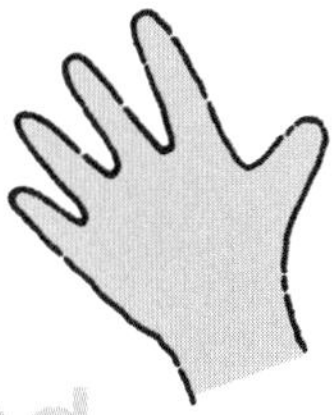 hard hand hold ___nd___	2. $2+2=4$ fact fast find ___	3.  chill chest child ___
4.  mark mass mask ___	5.  stand stump stamp ___	6.  belt best bent ___

Handwriting Helper

✎ Trace. Then write.

class

desks

chairs

teacher

📖 Ready, Set, READ!

Read. Then answer the questions.

Blue Food

Blueberries are small and round. They grow on a bush. One blueberry bush can grow many, many berries.

At first, blueberries are green and hard. Do not eat them yet. They need time to get bigger. Sun and rain will help them turn blue. Then they are **ripe** and ready to eat. Yum!

1. Which means the same as **ripe**?
   ○ A. all grown   ○ B. hard   ○ C. round

2. Why do blueberries need sun and rain?

_____

☺ BrainTeaser ☺

Write 1, 2, and 3 to show ABC order.

_____ salt	_____ pipe	_____ ox
_____ rice	_____ bug	_____ post
_____ moth	_____ worm	_____ both
_____ jump	_____ dance	_____ vote

Reading & Math Practice, Grade 1 © 2014 Scholastic Inc.

Number Place

Write the number that is 10 MORE.

9 _____   46 _____   54 _____

28 _____   87 _____   65 _____

FAST Math →

What time is it?

____ : ____   ____ : ____   ____ : ____   ____ : ____

Think Tank

There are 65 children who go ice skating. Then 12 of them go inside to rest. How many children keep skating?

_____ kids keep skating.

Show your work in the tank.

Data Place

Draw ✓ in the graph for each fruit you see.

How Many Fruits?

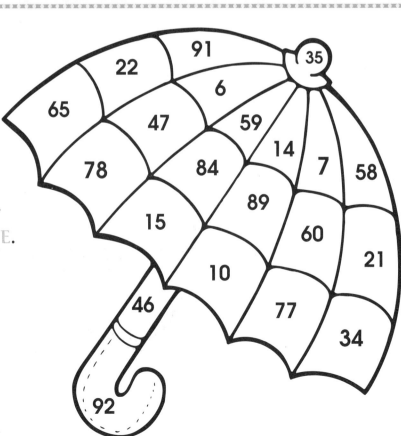

Apples	
Bananas	
Cherries	
Pears	

Key: ✓ = 1 piece of fruit

1. How many cherries? _____

2. Two fruits together equal the number of pears.

   They are _____ and _____ .

Puzzler

Color ODD numbers RED.
Color EVEN numbers BLUE.

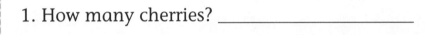
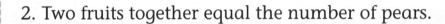

91 22 35 6 65 47 59 14 7 58 78 84 89 15 60 21 10 46 77 34 92

Reading & Math Practice, Grade 1 © 2014 Scholastic Inc.

FUN Phonics

Circle the word that names each picture. Write its <u>final</u> <u>blend</u>.

1.  wasp want walk _sp_	2.  best bird bend ___	3.  fort ford fork ___
4.  stink stunk skunk ___	5.  fact first fist ___	6.  pound paint pest ___

Handwriting Helper

✎ Trace. Then write.

read

write

spell

think

📖 Ready, Set, READ!

Read. Then answer the questions.

Swim Class

Peg did not know how to swim. She asked to go to a swim class. Her mom liked the idea. Peg starts today.

Peg gets to the pool on time. The class has ten kids and two teachers. One teacher helps Peg. Peg learns how to move her arms and legs. Peg and the teacher swim side by side.

1. Why did Peg want to go to swim class?

_____

_____

_____

_____

2. Peg had her class at a
   ○ A. lake
   ○ B. pool
   ○ C. beach

🌀 BrainTeaser 🌀

Use the picture clues to solve the puzzle.

ACROSS

1.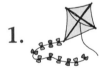

4.

5.

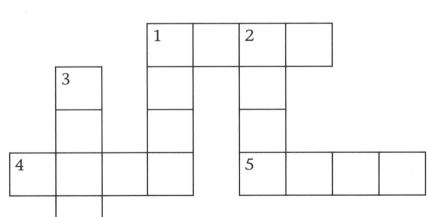

DOWN

1.

2

3.

Number Place

Write the number that is 10 LESS.

13 _____   74 _____   98 _____

61 _____   85 _____   72 _____

FAST Math

Draw hands on the clocks to show each time.

2:00

6:00

11:00

Think Tank

A zoo has 14 monkeys and 11 parrots. Each gets 1 apple a day. How many apples do all the animals eat in 2 days?

They eat _____ apples in all.

Show your work in the tank.

Data Place

Momo is a circus monkey.
He wears a hat and a vest.

• He has 1 purple hat and 1 red hat.

• He has 1 blue vest and 1 yellow vest.

Color each DIFFERENT outfit Momo can wear.

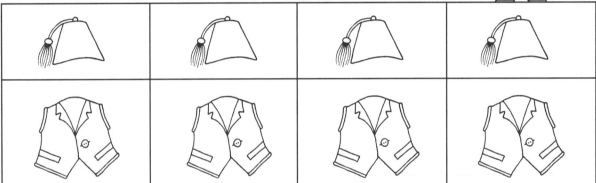

Puzzler

Connect the dots.
Start at 0.
Count by 10s.

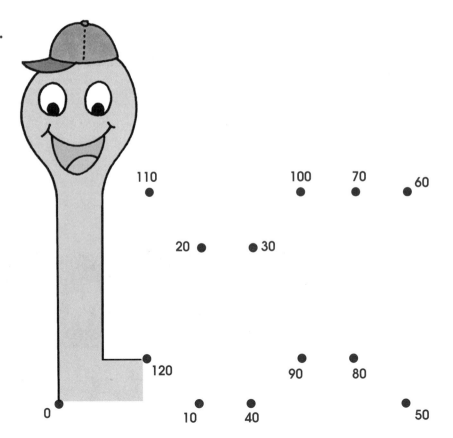

Reading & Math Practice, Grade 1 © 2014 Scholastic Inc.

FUN Phonics

**Write the missing digraph
for each word in the sentence.**

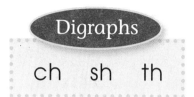

Digraphs

ch   sh   th

1. Mom is _____irty years old.

2. I like your new _____irt.

3. Do you like fried _____icken?

4. Please _____ut the door behind you.

5. Use an ax to _____op wood.

6. Can you _____ink of a joke?

Handwriting Helper

✎ **Trace. Then write.**

ice

river

water

creek

📖 Ready, Set, READ!

Read. Then answer the questions.

Arthur

Do you know the <u>Arthur</u> books? There are lots of them. But once, only two people knew Arthur.

Marc Brown made up Arthur. Mr. Brown was putting his son to bed. The boy asked for a story. Mr. Brown made up an animal named Arthur.

Marc Brown wrote his story as a book. The title was <u>Arthur's Nose</u>.

1. Another word for **title** is
    ○ A. author.   ○ B. book.   ○ C. name.

2. Who were the first people to know Arthur?

_____

🌀 BrainTeaser 🌀

Write **a**, **e**, **i**, **o**, or **u** to spell each animal name.

1. f _____ x   4. h _____ n

2. _____ nt   5. d _____ ck

3. fr _____ g   6. p _____ g

Reading & Math Practice, Grade 1 © 2014 Scholastic Inc.

Number Place

Match words and numbers.

twenty ●	● 80
forty ●	● 40
sixty ●	● 100
eighty ●	● 20
hundred ●	● 60

ten ●	● 90
thirty ●	● 10
fifty ●	● 70
seventy ●	● 30
ninety ●	● 50

FAST Math

What time is it?

____ : ____   ____ : ____   ____ : ____   ____ : ____

Think Tank

Tina has 6 coins. They are worth 50¢ in all. What coins does Tina have? Draw and label them.

Show your work in the tank.

Data Place

Use the calendar to answer the questions.

Weather in May

Sunday	Monday	Tuesday	Wednesday	Thursday	Friday	Saturday
1	2	3	4	5	6	7

1. How many days in a week? _____

2. How many days had ? _____

3. How many days had ? _____

4. What was the weather on Thursday? _____

5. Which were bad days for picnics? _____

_____

Puzzler

START with the number at the left.
Do what each arrow says. Use the key.
Write each NEW number.
Keep going to the end of the row.

Key

⇨ + 5

⇨ − 2

➡ − 10

53 ☐ ☐ ☐

86 ☐ ☐ ☐

Reading & Math Practice, Grade 1 © 2014 Scholastic Inc.

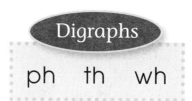
FUN Phonics

Write the missing digraph for each word in the sentence.

Digraphs

ph   th   wh

1. My bike has two _____eels.

2. Dad talks on his cell _____one.

3. _____en is it time for lunch?

4. Your ball is over _____ere.

5. Please take a _____oto of me!

6. I like _____is book a lot.

Handwriting Helper

✐ **Trace. Then write.**

pleased

big smile

so happy

very glad

📖 Ready, Set, READ!

Read. Then answer the questions.

Beads

Kim will make a necklace.
She has red, white, and blue beads.
She needs a loop of string.
It must fit over her head.
    Kim cuts white string.
Then she slips beads onto it.
She makes a pattern.
    Kim stops when the string
is nearly full. She ties up the ends.
All done!

1. Kim will wear her beads around her
    ○ A. waist   ○ B. wrist   ○ C. neck

2. What colors does Kim use?

_____

🌀 BrainTeaser 🌀

Write **a**, **e**, **i**, **o**, or **u** to spell each color.

1. bl _____ ck

2. br _____ wn

3. gr _____ n

4. bl _____ e

5. y _____ ll _____ w

6. p _____ nk

Reading & Math Practice, Grade 1 © 2014 Scholastic Inc.

Number Place

How many dimes?

20 pennies = _____ dimes

30 pennies = _____ dimes

40 pennies = _____ dimes

60 pennies = _____ dimes

80 pennies = _____ dimes

90 pennies = _____ dimes

FAST Math

Draw hands on the clocks to show each time.

10:30

5:30

9:00

Think Tank

Three kids count steps from the door to their seats. Lia takes 15 steps. Pam takes 4 steps less than Lia. Ari takes 6 more steps than Pam. Who is nearest the door?

_____ is nearest.

Show your work in the tank.

Data Place

Plan a perfect day.
On the chart, draw or write what
you would do at each time of day.

Wake up	Morning	Noon	Afternoon	Night

Puzzler

Color squares to make
an animal on this grid.

Color squares to make
a pattern on this grid.

Reading & Math Practice, Grade 1 © 2014 Scholastic Inc.

FUN Phonics

Write the name for each picture. Listen for the **ng** sound.

1.  _____	2. 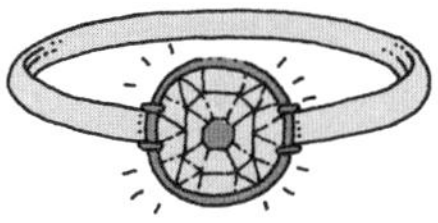 _____	3.  _____
4.  _____	5.  _____	6.  _____

Handwriting Helper

✏️ Trace. Then write.

unhappy

all alone

felt blue

sad to say

📖 Ready, Set, READ!

Read. Then answer the questions.

Not Like Its Name

A jellyfish is not a fish. It is
a sea animal. It is not made of jelly.
It is made mostly of water.

Some jellyfish are as clear as glass.
Others have colors. All are soft and
mushy. They come in all sizes.

A jellyfish has many arms.
They hang down like soft ribbons.
But the soft arms can sting. Stay away!

1. Jellyfish are made mostly of
   ○ A. jelly   ○ B. fish   ○ C. water

2. Why should you stay away from them?

_____

🌀 BrainTeaser 🌀

Read each title. Circle fiction or fact.

1. How to Build a Go-Cart   **fiction** or **fact**

2. The Singing Noodle   **fiction** or **fact**

3. Dragons at School   **fiction** or **fact**

4. Grow Your Own Corn   **fiction** or **fact**

Reading & Math Practice, Grade 1 © 2014 Scholastic Inc.

Number Place

Round to the nearest 10¢.

17¢ → ____ ¢   32¢ → ____ ¢   56¢ → ____ ¢   78¢ → ____ ¢

44¢ → ____ ¢   65¢ → ____ ¢   81¢ → ____ ¢   93¢ → ____ ¢

FAST Math

Add.

$$\begin{array}{r} 24 \\ + \ 32 \\ \hline \end{array} \qquad \begin{array}{r} 63 \\ + \ 14 \\ \hline \end{array} \qquad \begin{array}{r} 48 \\ + \ 51 \\ \hline \end{array} \qquad \begin{array}{r} 56 \\ + \ 23 \\ \hline \end{array} \qquad \begin{array}{r} 32 \\ + \ 45 \\ \hline \end{array} \qquad \begin{array}{r} 70 \\ + \ 17 \\ \hline \end{array}$$

Think Tank

Cody's favorite TV show starts at 7:30. It lasts one half-hour. What time does it say on Cody's clock when the show ends?

Write the time in numbers on the clock.

Data Place

Look at the ruler. Then draw each line. Start at ● .

	1	2	3	4	5	6

Draw a line about 3 inches long.

○ ●

Draw a line about 5 inches long.

○ ●

Draw a line less than 2 inches long.

○ ●

Order the lines from 1 (longest) to 3 (shortest).
Write the numbers in the circles.

Puzzler

Jin got a new piggy bank. His dad will give him
pennies for it each day. Here is his plan.

Which day?	1	2	3	4	5	6	7
How many pennies?	1	2	4	8	16		

Figure out Dad's pattern. How many
pennies will Jin get on Day 6? On Day 7?

Write the numbers in the table.

Reading & Math Practice, Grade 1 © 2014 Scholastic Inc.

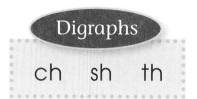
FUN Phonics

Write the missing digraph for each word in the sentence.

Digraphs

ch   sh   th

1. Let's all sit on the cou_____ .

2. Paper money is called ca_____ .

3. Deb has her first loose too_____ .

4. He will wa_____ the dirty pans.

5. Spring starts in the mon_____ of March.

6. We had fruit pun_____ at the party.

Handwriting Helper

✎ **Trace. Then write.**

question

quick nap

quiet time

Queen May

📖 Ready, Set, READ!

Read. Then answer the questions.

Help!

"Help!" said the fly on the wall.

"Where are you?" asked Tina.

"I am up here," yelled the fly.

Tina looked up to see a talking fly.

"Flies cannot talk!" she said.

"I can," said the fly. "I must!
I am stuck in your room. I cannot get out.
Will you please open the window?"

"Okay," said Tina. "You said, **please**."

1. What was odd about the fly?
   ○ A. It was inside.   ○ B. It could speak.

2. Why did Tina help the fly?

_____

🌀 BrainTeaser 🌀

Write a sentence that uses each word.

1. **elbow** _____

_____

2. **sticky** _____

_____

Number Place

Round to the nearest number of dimes.

37¢ → _____ dimes   42¢ → _____ dimes   66¢ → _____ dimes

54¢ → _____ dimes   75¢ → _____ dimes   91¢ → _____ dimes

FAST Math

Round each addend to the nearest 10. Estimate the sum.

47 → ☐   22 → ☐   61 → ☐

+ 31 → ☐   + 59 → ☐   + 17 → ☐
_____   _____   _____

about: _____   about: _____   about: _____

Think Tank

Mr. Lim has 28 children in his class. There are 15 boys. How many children are girls? There are

_____ girls.

Show your work in the tank.

Data Place

Three friends counted birds at the lake.

Add or subtract to find the missing numbers.

	Ducks	Swans	Total
Roscoe	16	3	
Noah	17		22
Kerry		6	19

1. Noah saw _____ ducks.

2. _____ saw 6 swans.

3. Roscoe saw _____ birds in all.

4. Who counted the fewest ducks? _____

Puzzler

This is a number puzzle.

• Each row ⟷
  needs a 1, 2, 3, and 4.

• Each column ↕
  needs a 1, 2, 3, and 4.

• Numbers can be in any order.

Write the missing numbers.

2	1	4	3
4			1
1			4
3	4	1	2

Reading & Math Practice, Grade 1 © 2014 Scholastic Inc.

FUN Phonics

Fill in the chart. Add -**ing** and -**ed** to each word.
One row is done for you.

Base Word	-ing	-ed
1. show	showing	showed
2. lick		
3. plant		
4. brush		
5. spell		
6. play		

Handwriting Helper

✎ Trace. Then write.

zipper

zigzag

zoom off

zero in

📖 Ready, Set, READ!

Read. Then answer the questions.

Crayon Museum

You can have a great time
at the crayon museum!
You can learn about art.
You can watch crayons get made.
You can see and smell hot wax
in many colors. The wax gets hard
to turn into crayons.

You can make art there, too.
You can make shadow art with your body
at Cool Moves. You can draw
on the sidewalks at Chalk Walk.

red

green

yellow

blue

1. What do you make art with at Cool Moves?

○ A. crayons   ○ B. chalk   ○ C. shadows

2. What are crayons made of? _____

🌀 BrainTeaser 🌀

Write a question that uses each word.

1. **ice** _____

_____

2. **frog** _____

_____

Reading & Math Practice, Grade 1 © 2014 Scholastic Inc.

Number Place

Round to the nearest ten.

16 → ____   21 → ____   45 → ____   67 → ____

33 → ____   54 → ____   71 → ____   88 → ____

FAST Math

Round each number to the nearest 10. Estimate the difference.

$$49 \rightarrow \boxed{}$$
$$- \ 31 \rightarrow \boxed{}$$

about: _____

$$72 \rightarrow \boxed{}$$
$$- \ 29 \rightarrow \boxed{}$$

about: _____

$$86 \rightarrow \boxed{}$$
$$- \ 13 \rightarrow \boxed{}$$

about: _____

Think Tank

Finish each day name. Order the days from 1 to 7.
Count Sunday as Day 1. Write the numbers in the boxes.

☐ F r __ __ __ __ __   ☐ T u e __ __ __ __ __

☐ M o __ __ __ __ __   ☐ T h u r __ __ __ __ __

☐ S a t __ __ __ __ __   ☐ W e d n e s __ __ __ __

☐ S u __ __ __ __ __

Data Place

Renee has $10. She goes to the movies.

Use the price list to answer the questions.

<table>
<tr><td>PRICES</td></tr>
<tr><td>Child's Ticket . . . . . . $5</td></tr>
<tr><td>Large Popcorn . . . . $3</td></tr>
<tr><td>Small Popcorn. . . . . $2</td></tr>
<tr><td>Large Soda . . . . $2</td></tr>
<tr><td>Small Soda . . . . $1</td></tr>
</table>

1. How much money does Renee have

   after she buys a ticket? _____

2. Her dad told her to bring home $1.

   But Renee wants popcorn and soda.

   What can she order? _____

   _____

3. How much would it cost for 4 children to buy

   movie tickets? _____

Puzzler

Write EVERY 2-digit number you can. Use the 3 numbers in the boxes ONLY. Try for all 6 numbers.

| 8 | 2 | 4 |

Circle the greatest number. Underline the least number.

158

Reading & Math Practice, Grade 1 © 2014 Scholastic Inc.

FUN Phonics

Fill in the chart. Add -**ing** and -**ed** to each word.
One row is done for you.

Base Word	-ing	-ed
1. chew	chew**ing**	chew**ed**
2. mix		
3. reach		
4. part		
5. need		
6. jump		

Handwriting Helper

✎ Trace. Then write.

joker

join in

jellyroll

juggle

📖 Ready, Set, READ!

Read. Then answer the questions.

Two Dollars

Chet wants a pet. He takes two dollars to the pet shop. "Hi," Chet says. "I have two dollars. What pet can I get?"

The shop man says, "You can get one mouse. Or you can get two fish."

"Two fish, please," says Chet. The man puts two fish in a bag of water. Now Chet has two pets!

1. What did Chet want at first?

   ○ A. money   ○ B. fish   ○ C. a pet

2. Why did the fish go into a bag of water?

   _____

🌀 BrainTeaser 🌀

Write a sentence about each picture.

_____

_____

_____

_____

Reading & Math Practice, Grade 1 © 2014 Scholastic Inc.

Number Place

Regroup 10 ones as 1 ten.

3 tens 12 ones = ___4___ tens ___2___ ones

4 tens 15 ones = _____ tens _____ ones

5 tens 19 ones = _____ tens _____ ones

6 tens 17 ones = _____ tens _____ ones

FAST Math

Subtract.

64	78	83	95	52	44
− 33	− 16	− 71	− 23	− 12	− 21
_____	_____	_____	_____	_____	_____

Think Tank

Shari made up a number pattern. Write the next 3 numbers.

Show your work in the tank.

98, 87, 76, 65, 54,

_____ , _____ , _____ ,

Data Place

Some first graders took out library books.

Graph the data in the table.

Let  stand for 1 book.

Child	Books
Jamila	3
Opal	6
Riley	4

Books Taken Out

Jamila	
Opal	
Riley	

Key: ▢ = 1 book

Puzzler

Get the rocket to the moon!
Count by 2s from 2 to 50.
Shade the boxes as you go.

53	48	51	43	57		
50	46	49	51	23		
51	45	44	49	15		
43	42	63	65	7	11	93
39	41	40	31	53	13	6	1	3
37	38	35	23	11	8	5	4	**2**
36	26	24	22	21	9	10		
34	28	25	20	15	13	12		
32	30	23	18	16	14	11		

Reading & Math Practice, Grade 1 © 2014 Scholastic Inc.

FUN Phonics

Fill in the chart.

Add -**er** and -**est** to each word.

One row is done for you.

Base Word	-er	-est
1. fast	faster	fastest
2. old		
3. tall		
4. high		
5. young		

Handwriting Helper

✎ Trace. Then write.

ox cart

textbook

Exit sign

six foxes

📖 Ready, Set, READ!

Read. Then answer the questions.

Young Inventor

Abbey Fleck was eight years old. She and her dad were cooking bacon. Then the paper towels ran out. How could they drain off the fat?

Abbey got an idea. A little rack might hold bacon up as it cooked. A tray below would catch the fat.

Abbey tried hard. Soon she made her idea work. She called it the "Makin' Bacon" dish.

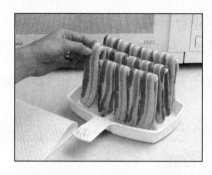

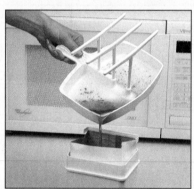

1. Which happened first?
   - ○ A. Abbey got an idea.
   - ○ B. Paper towels ran out.
   - ○ C. Abbey and Dad made bacon.

2. How many rows of bacon can the rack hold?

_____

🌀 BrainTeaser 🌀

Finish each sentence.

1. Kim looked for her lost _____.

2. Zack ran after his _____.

3. Chad hid behind a _____.

4. Ana swam in the _____.

Number Place

Order the numbers from LEAST to GREATEST.

70, 55, 67 _____

62, 55, 66 _____

94, 49, 50 _____

118, 75, 104 _____

FAST Math

Add. Regroup 10 ones as 1 ten.

$$
\begin{array}{r} 33 \\ +\ 37 \\ \hline \end{array}
\qquad
\begin{array}{r} 54 \\ +\ 16 \\ \hline \end{array}
\qquad
\begin{array}{r} 22 \\ +\ 28 \\ \hline \end{array}
\qquad
\begin{array}{r} 55 \\ +\ 35 \\ \hline \end{array}
\qquad
\begin{array}{r} 12 \\ +\ 48 \\ \hline \end{array}
\qquad
\begin{array}{r} 61 \\ +\ 19 \\ \hline \end{array}
$$

Think Tank

Here's a tricky riddle: How many 1s are on a clock face?

Draw a picture in the tank to help you solve the riddle.

Data Place

How many veggies did Vicki pick?

**Count and tally them.
Then write the number.**

Vicki's Veggies

Veggie	Tally	Number
Carrots		4
Peppers		
Potatoes		

1. Vicki picked the most _____ .

2. Vicki picked 4 _____ .

3. She picked _____ veggies in all.

Puzzler

Each ◇ = 1 dart.

Write the score each dartboard shows.

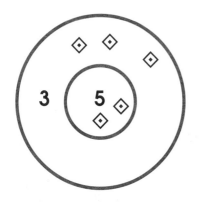

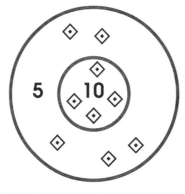

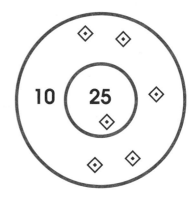

Score: _____   Score: _____   Score: _____

Reading & Math Practice, Grade 1 © 2014 Scholastic Inc.

FUN Phonics

A **compound** word is made up of two short words.
Write the compound word for each picture.

1. sun + flower = _____

2. dog + house = _____

3. flash + light = _____

4. scare + crow = _____

5. wheel + chair = _____

Handwriting Helper

✏ Trace. Then write.

on tiptoes

Hurry up.

Hop along.

Walk fast.

Reading & Math Practice, Grade 1 © 2014 Scholastic Inc.

📖 Ready, Set, READ!

Read. Then answer the questions.

Kitten

I wish I had a nickel.
I wish I had a dime.
I wish I had a kitten
to kiss me all the time.

Mom gave me a nickel.
Dad gave me a dime.
Gus gave me a kitten
to kiss me all the time.

I don't miss the nickel.
I don't miss the dime.
Now I have a kitten
to kiss me all the time!

1. Who had a wish?

   ○ A. a kitten   ○ B. a child   ○ C. a parent

2. Who made the wish come true?

🌀 BrainTeaser 🌀

Try to spell it!

 _____

 _____

Reading & Math Practice, Grade 1 © 2014 Scholastic Inc.

Number Place

Order the numbers from GREATEST to LEAST.

41, 33, 28 _____

49, 59, 39 _____

83, 33, 38 _____

105, 117, 99 _____

FAST Math

Add. Regroup when needed.

$$\begin{array}{r} 41 \\ + \ 28 \\ \hline \end{array} \qquad \begin{array}{r} 24 \\ + \ 26 \\ \hline \end{array} \qquad \begin{array}{r} 46 \\ + \ 24 \\ \hline \end{array} \qquad \begin{array}{r} 11 \\ + \ 33 \\ \hline \end{array} \qquad \begin{array}{r} 26 \\ + \ 51 \\ \hline \end{array} \qquad \begin{array}{r} 43 \\ + \ 17 \\ \hline \end{array}$$

_____ _____ _____ _____ _____ _____

Think Tank

Show half of each square in the tank.

• Draw a RED line to show half one way.

• Draw a BLUE line to show half a different way.

Reading & Math Practice, Grade 1 © 2014 Scholastic Inc.

Data Place

Lizzy brushes her hair each day. She counts the brushstrokes:

Monday	60
Tuesday	40
Wednesday	40
Thursday	50
Friday	30

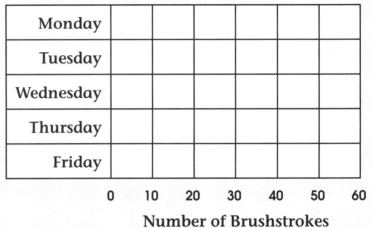

Brushstrokes for Lizzy

Monday						
Tuesday						
Wednesday						
Thursday						
Friday						

0   10   20   30   40   50   60

Number of Brushstrokes

Color bars to show Lizzy's brushstrokes each day.

Find the difference between MOST and LEAST strokes. _____

Puzzler

Write **H** for HALVES. Write **F** for FOURTHS.

170

Reading & Math Practice, Grade 1 © 2014 Scholastic Inc.

FUN Phonics

A **compound** word is made up of two short words. Complete the compound word that names each picture. Use the word bank.

Word Bank

boat	cage
fish	robe
corn	bug

1. lady_____	2. bath_____	3. bird_____
4. sail_____	5. pop_____	6. star_____

Handwriting Helper

✎ Trace. Then write.

Speak up!

Say cheese!

Sit down.

📖 Ready, Set, READ!

Read. Then answer the questions.

Car Wash Day

Mom parks the car near the hose.
She rolls the windows up tight.
I fill a pail with water and soap.

Next I use the hose to wet the car.
Mom and I rub with big sponges.
Then I spray off the soap.

Last, we wipe away the water
with old rags. We are dirty and wet,
but the car is clean and dry!

1. What are the rags for?
   ○ A. washing   ○ B. drying   ○ C. spraying

2. Why does Mom roll up the windows?

_____

⑨ BrainTeaser ⑥

Try to spell it!

_____

_____

Number Place

Write in number form.

thirty-three _____   eighty-six _____

seventy-five _____   forty-one _____

ninety-nine _____   fifteen _____

FAST Math

Subtract. Regroup 1 ten as 10 ones.

50	80	90	70	40	60
− 18	− 27	− 32	− 36	− 28	− 11
_____	_____	_____	_____	_____	_____

Think Tank

Draw some coins to make 41¢. Use ONLY dimes, nickels, and pennies. Write the value on each coin.

Show your work in the tank.

Data Place

Finish the table. Draw tallies or write numbers.

Books Read Last Week

Books Read	Tally	Number of People
0	II	
1		6
2		9
3							

1. How many people read NO books? _____

2. How many people read 1 book? _____

3. How many books did 9 people read? _____

Puzzler

Use the key to solve the problems.

Key

| 11 | 22 | 60 | 75 | 99 |

1. ⬭ + ⬡ = _____

2. ☾ + ☆ = _____

3. ☾ – ⬭ = _____

4. ☁ – ☾ = _____

Reading & Math Practice, Grade 1 © 2014 Scholastic Inc.

FUN Phonics

A **compound** word is made up of two short words. Complete the compound word that names each picture. Use the word bank.

Word Bank

plane	foot
cake	lunch
rain	pack

1. back_____	2. _____coat	3. cup_____
4. _____box	5. air_____	6. _____ball

Handwriting Helper

✎ Trace. Then write.

Draw a toy.

Sing a song.

Paint a bird.

📖 Ready, Set, READ!

Read. Then answer the questions.

Worms

Q: What is a worm?

A: A worm is an animal with no legs or bones. It has a mouth but no teeth.

Q: Where do worms live?

A: They live in soil. They dig for food. They cannot live in hot or frozen places.

Q: How do worms move?

A: Worms wiggle bit by bit. Little hairs on their bodies help them inch along.

1. Which does a worm have?
   ○ A. teeth   ○ B. hairs   ○ C. legs

2. Where do worms live?

_____

⊚ BrainTeaser ⊚

Write **?** for a question. Write **!** to show surprise.

1. Is there room_____

2. Oh, my gosh_____

3. Who is she_____

4. I won the prize_____

Reading & Math Practice, Grade 1 © 2014 Scholastic Inc.

Number Place

Write the number that comes BETWEEN.

38, ____, 40   27, ____, 29   42, ____, 44

63, ____, 65   16, ____, 18   51, ____, 53

45, ____, 47   99, ____, 101   70, ____, 72

FAST Math

Subtract. Regroup when needed.

$$\begin{array}{r} 49 \\ -\ 16 \\ \hline \end{array} \qquad \begin{array}{r} 70 \\ -\ 36 \\ \hline \end{array} \qquad \begin{array}{r} 67 \\ -\ 27 \\ \hline \end{array} \qquad \begin{array}{r} 82 \\ -\ 31 \\ \hline \end{array} \qquad \begin{array}{r} 98 \\ -\ 23 \\ \hline \end{array} \qquad \begin{array}{r} 90 \\ -\ 68 \\ \hline \end{array}$$

Think Tank

Arun is 19 years old. Ree is 13 years old. How many years younger is Ree than Arun?

Ree is _____ years younger.

Show your work in the tank.

Reading & Math Practice, Grade 1 © 2014 Scholastic Inc.

Data Place

Kids voted on best things to do at a fair.

Use the chart to answer the questions at right.

What to Do	Votes
Face Painting	15
Spin Art	9
Ring Toss	11
Fun Nails	6

1. What did 11 kids want to do?

   _____

2. What got the most votes?

   _____

3. How many more voted for Spin Art than Fun Nails?

   _____

4. Find the difference between MOST and FEWEST votes.

   _____

Puzzler

Connect the dots.
Start at 120.
Count back by 10s.

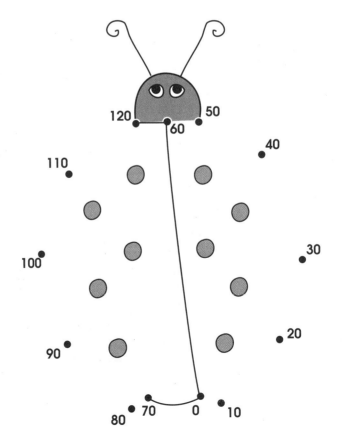

Reading & Math Practice, Grade 1 © 2014 Scholastic Inc.

FUN Phonics

Draw lines to match the two words to the **contraction** that means the same. Look for ' where a letter was.

I am •	• It's
She is •	• You're
It is •	• She's
We are •	• They're
You are •	• We're
They are •	• I'm

Handwriting Helper

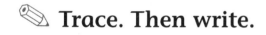 Trace. Then write.

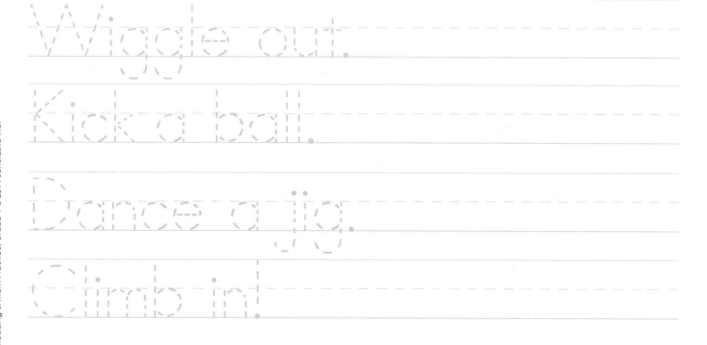

Wiggle out.

Kick a ball.

Dance a jig.

Climb in.

📖 Ready, Set, READ!

Read. Then answer the questions.

Army Ants

Army ants move in big groups.
They march together to find food.
Nothing stops them. Not even big holes.
Some army ants team up.
They hook legs to make a chain.
More ants hook on. The chain grows.
The ant chain soon reaches across
the hole. It's like a bridge. Other ants
cross it.
At last the ants unhook and march on.

1. Army ants are special because they move
   ○ A. slowly.   ○ B. in water.   ○ C. in big groups.

2. How do the ants team up?

_____

🌀 BrainTeaser 🌀

Write three words that
start with **sh**.

Write three words that
end with **sh**.

_____   _____

_____   _____

_____   _____

Reading & Math Practice, Grade 1 © 2014 Scholastic Inc.

Number Place

Compare. Write **<** or **>**.

68 ◯ 86   37 ◯ 17   24 ◯ 42

75 ◯ 69   98 ◯ 89   88 ◯ 91

FAST Math

Add or subtract. Watch the signs!

```
   55          64          76          41          37          98
 - 14        + 34        - 26        + 37        + 52        - 76
 ____        ____        ____        ____        ____        ____
```

Think Tank

1 hour = 60 minutes

How many minutes are in half an hour? Use mental math to solve. Half an hour has

_____ minutes.

Use the tank if you need to.

Data Place

Finish the table.

First Graders at Moss School

Class	Girls	Boys	Total
1A		14	27
1B	14	14	
1C	14		27

1. Which is the biggest class? _____

2. Which class has the fewest girls? _____

3. Finish the sentence: Classes 1A and 1C both have

_____

_____

Puzzler

Write the letter to make each number sentence true.

A = 10	E = 20	I = 30	O = 40	U = 50

$24 + $ _____ $= 54$

$100 - $ _____ $= 60$

_____ $- 25 = 25$

$69 + $ _____ $= 79$

_____ $+ 16 = 56$

$48 - 28 = $ _____

182

Reading & Math Practice, Grade 1 © 2014 Scholastic Inc.

FUN Phonics

Draw lines to match the two words to the **contraction** that means the same. Look for ' where the letters **wi** were.

Contract means to <u>get</u> <u>smaller</u>.

I will •	• It'll
He will •	• You'll
It will •	• I'll
We will •	• They'll
You will •	• We'll
They will •	• He'll

Handwriting Helper

✎ Trace. Then write.

red cheeks

long legs

two feet

cold toes

📖 Ready, Set, READ!

Read. Then answer the questions.

Cleanup Day

It's cleanup day. Dad turns work into fun. We get rags and mops. We get bottles of cleaner. We are ready!

Dad and I dust and dance. We make faces as we mop. We wiggle when we wipe. We act silly but we work hard.

Soon Dad and I are done. We wash up and change clothes. Then it's time for ice cream!

1. Cleanup Day is fun because Dad gets
   ○ A. busy   ○ B. silly   ○ C. quiet

2. What is the treat when they finish?

_____

🌀 BrainTeaser 🌀

Use all the words to make a sentence.

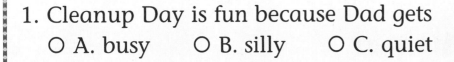

dry.   It   hot   and   is

1. _____

too   apple   soft.   is   My

2. _____

Number Place

Sort the numbers.
Write them where
they belong.

| 86 | 8 | 63 | 95 | 39 | 48 | 12 | 31 |
| 0 | 77 | 26 | 81 | 17 | 89 | 40 | |

Less Than 20	Between 21 and 50	Greater Than 50

FAST Math

Add or subtract. Watch the signs!

```
  67        25        76        49        56        87
- 36      + 35      + 13      - 28      + 34      - 57
____      ____      ____      ____      ____      ____
```

Think Tank

A hammer is 9 inches
long. An ax is 18 inches
long. How much longer
is the ax? Draw a
picture to compare
them. The ax is

_____ inches longer.

Show your work
in the tank.

Data Place

Ann Ben Fritz Dawn Ella Carl Gina Henry

Sort the children by what they are wearing.
Write their names where they belong in the Venn diagram.

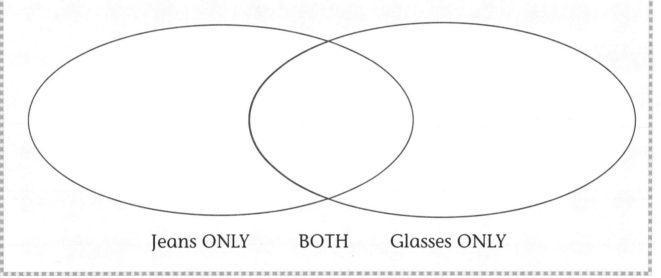

Jeans ONLY   BOTH   Glasses ONLY

Puzzler

Count the blocks in each figure.
Count ALL the blocks, even hidden ones.

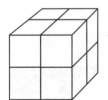

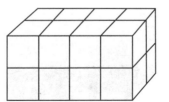

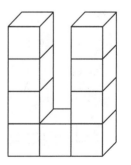

_____   _____   _____

Reading & Math Practice, Grade 1 © 2014 Scholastic Inc.

FUN Phonics

Write the **contraction** that fits each sentence.
Use the word bank.

Word Bank

aren't
can't
doesn't
don't
isn't

1. It **is not** right to lie. _____

2. They **do not** eat pork. _____

3. We **are not** ready. _____

4. I **cannot** see a thing. _____

5. She **does not** like it. _____

Handwriting Helper

✏ Trace. Then write.

child's play

check off

chop wood.

cheer up.

📖 Ready, Set, READ!

Read. Then answer the questions.

Watch Out!

Poison ivy is a plant. It grows
in the woods, near roads, and by fields.
Poison ivy leaves have an oil in them.
The oil gives people a bad skin rash.
The rash itches. It takes days to go away.
Learn how poison ivy looks. If you
touch it, you'll be sorry! Remember this:

Leaves of three? Let it be!

1. Poison ivy is

    ○ A. an oil   ○ B. a plant   ○ C. a rash

2. How will you feel if you touch poison ivy?

_____

🌀 BrainTeaser 🌀

Circle the word that means the **same**.

shout		silly		quick	
ask	yell	goofy	right	slow	fast

sound		alike		middle	
noise	smell	love	same	end	center

Number Place

Write how many tens and ones.

72 = _____ tens _____ ones   90 = _____ tens _____ ones

89 = _____ tens _____ ones   63 = _____ tens _____ ones

24 = _____ tens _____ ones   31 = _____ tens _____ ones

FAST Math

Round to the nearest dime. Estimate the sum.

57¢ → ☐   32¢ → ☐   43¢ → ☐

+ 22¢ → ☐   + 49¢ → ☐   +38¢ → ☐
_____   _____   _____

about: _____ ¢   about: _____ ¢   about: _____ ¢

Think Tank

Rex is a dog. He hid some bones in his yard. Rex hid more than 5 bones, but fewer than 8 bones. Rex did NOT hide 6 bones. How many bones did Rex hide? Rex hid

_____ bones.

Show your work in the tank.

Reading & Math Practice, Grade 1 © 2014 Scholastic Inc.

Data Place

These are the longest names in Amy's class.

Varastadt Bagdazarian — called Vara
Annabella Giangregorio — called Anna
Shakuntala Satapathy — called Tala

Fill in the table about the names.

Child	Letters in First Name	Letters in Last Name	Total Number of Letters
Vara			
Anna			
Tala			

1. Who has the longest first name? _____

2. Who has the longest last name? _____

3. Who has the longest full name? _____

Puzzler

Look at the 2 lines.
Which is longer?
Use a ruler to know for sure.

What did you find out? _____

_____

FUN Phonics

Read each word pair. Circle pairs that rhyme.

1. fix	fox		2. plate	wait
3. send	blend		4. knows	road
5. march	porch		6. fry	tie
7. goat	note		8. stick	shock
9. jeep	sleep		10. fudge	bridge

Handwriting Helper

✎ Trace. Then write.

shipshape

short story

shiny shoes

shy sheep

📖 Ready, Set, READ!

Read. Then answer the questions.

Lion and Mouse   A Fable

Lion was asleep. Mouse ran up his tail and woke him. "Stop!" roared Lion. "I will eat you, bad Mouse."

"Sorry!" cried Mouse. "Please free me. I will help you later." Lion **yawned**. He let Mouse go.

That night, Lion fell into a net. He was stuck. Mouse heard Lion roar. He ran to help. Mouse chewed the net to set Lion free.

1. What does the word **yawned** tell about Lion?
   - ○ A. He was hungry.
   - ○ B. He was tired.
   - ○ C. He was yelling.

2. What does the story teach?
   - ○ A. Never wake a lion.
   - ○ B. Stay away from nets.
   - ○ C. Kind acts can be returned.

🌀 BrainTeaser 🌀

Circle the word that means the **opposite**.

sad		fast		awake	
happy	blue	first	slow	asleep	about

stand		break		push	
reach	sit	fix	brake	drag	pull

Reading & Math Practice, Grade 1 © 2014 Scholastic Inc.

Number Place

Write the number that is 10 MORE.

64 _____   35 _____   71 _____

57 _____   88 _____   46 _____

Write the number that is 10 LESS.

35 _____   92 _____   67 _____

14 _____   43 _____   58 _____

FAST Math

Round to the nearest dime. Estimate the difference.

58¢ → ☐   82¢ → ☐   93¢ → ☐

– 31¢ → ☐   – 49¢ → ☐   – 57¢ → ☐

about: _____ ¢   about: _____ ¢   about: _____ ¢

Think Tank

A field mouse ate 4 wild onions, 5 grapes, and 6 acorns. How many pieces of food did the mouse eat?

_____ pieces of food

Show your work in the tank.

Data Place

Best at the Playground

Jungle Gym	👍 👍 👍 👍 👍
Swing	👍 👍 👍 👍
Seesaw	👍 👍 👍 👍 👍 👍 👍

Key: 👍 = 1 vote

Use the graph to answer the questions.

1. Five people voted for _____ .

2. Which playground place got the most votes? _____

3. Which got the fewest votes? _____

4. How many children voted? _____

Puzzler

Pretend to pick up both objects.
Circle the one that weighs more.

1.    or   2.   or

3.   or   4.    or

FUN Phonics

Read each word. Write it in the chart where it goes.

brain   click   flat   grape   mile   pill   shine   track

Short a	Long a	Short i	Long i

Handwriting Helper

✎ Trace. Then write.

The Lorax

The Mitten

Owl Moon

Swimmy

📖 Ready, Set, READ!

Read. Then answer the questions.

Happy Clams?

"As happy as a clam" is a saying.
But why do people say it? The full saying
is "as happy as a clam **at high tide**."
So let's think about clams and tides.

   At **low tide** the water is not deep.
It is when people dig up clams to eat.

   At **high tide** the water is deep.
It covers the clams. They are safe.
No wonder they are happy then!

1. People dig up clams to
   ○ A. help them   ○ B. tickle them   ○ C. eat them

2. Water is deep at _____ tide.

🌀 BrainTeaser 🌀

Fill in a word that makes sense.

1. Penny forgot to _____ her book.

2. The cows go into the _____.

3. Hank hates to eat_____.

4. Will you be my _____?

Reading & Math Practice, Grade 1 © 2014 Scholastic Inc.

Number Place

Write 4 different numbers in each cloud.

| Less Than 25 | Between 26 and 75 | Greater Than 76 |

FAST Math

X the equations that are FALSE.

| 4 + 7 = 47 | 12 − 6 = 18 | 8 + 8 = 16 |
| 7 + 8 = 15 | 40 + 60 = 100 | 20 − 10 = 30 |

💡 Think Tank

Mario made a round pizza. Draw lines to show how to cut his pizza into FOURTHS. How do you know how many pieces to make?

Show your work in the tank.

Data Place

Tally and write the number for every letter in this tongue twister.

> Ted fed Fred bread.

Letter	Tally	Number
a		
b		
d		
e		
f		
r		
t		

Puzzler

Pretend to fill both objects.
Circle the one that holds more.

1. or

2.  or

3. or

4. or

FUN Phonics

Read each word. Write it in the chart where it goes.

blond   dream   edge   flock   roast   seen   test   whole

Short e	Long e	Short o	Long o

Handwriting Helper

✎ **Trace. Then write.**

Oh, Susanna

Looby Loo

Shoo Fly

Hokey Pokey

📖 Ready, Set, READ!

Read. Then answer the questions.

Animals of the Desert

The sun **glares**. The desert is dry and very hot. How do animals stay alive there?

A desert fox has big ears that give off heat. They help to keep the fox cool. Snakes and lizards like the heat. They spend the day in the hot sun.

But the sun is too hot for many animals. They stay underground. At night, they leave their holes to look for food.

1. The word **glares** means
   ○ A. is cold.   ○ B. shines brightly.   ○ C. goes away.

2. Why do some desert animals hunt at night?

_____

🌀 BrainTeaser 🌀

Make as many words as you can. Use ONLY the letters in the wheel. Each word must have an **E**, plus two or more letters.

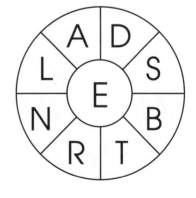

_____

_____

_____

Number Place

Write the missing numbers.

77, _____ , _____ , _____ , _____ , 82

49, _____ , _____ , _____ , _____ , 54

98, _____ , _____ , _____ , _____ , 103

FAST Math

Write the missing number to make the equation TRUE.

☐ − 8 = 6	☐ + 10 = 20	18 − ☐ = 10
20 + ☐ = 30	15 = ☐ + 10	20 = ☐ − 2

Think Tank

Write every DIFFERENT addition fact you know that equals 10.

Show your work in the tank.

Data Place

January in Oswego, New York, in 1966 was very snowy.
The calendar shows when snow fell.

Use the calendar to answer the questions.

Sunday	Monday	Tuesday	Wednesday	Thursday	Friday	Saturday
25	26	27	28	29	30	31
Snow: 0 inches	Snow: 0 inches	Snow: 8 inches	Snow: 12 inches	Snow: 11 inches	Snow: 21 inches	Snow: 50 inches

1. When did the snow start to fall? _____

2. How many days in a row got snow? _____

3. How much snow fell in all on Wednesday,

   Thursday, and Friday? _____

4. Was this more or less than the amount of snow

   that fell on January 31? _____

Puzzler

Write the second part of each math word.
Use the letter bank to help.

1. e _____

2. hun _____

3. num _____

4. quar _____

5. twen _____

6. ze _____

Letter Bank

ro
ty
ter
ber
qual
dred

Reading & Math Practice, Grade 1 © 2014 Scholastic Inc.

FUN Phonics

Synonyms mean the same. Match each word on the left with its synonym on the right.

tired •   • pull

pick •   • mend

drag •   • choose

jump •   • tale

fix •   • sleepy

story •   • leap

Handwriting Helper

✎ Trace. Then write.

How are you?

I am fine.

📖 Ready, Set, READ!

Read. Then answer the questions.

Why Bears Have Short Tails

Bear met Fox in the woods one winter day. Fox had many tasty fish.

"How can I get fish?" asked Bear.

Fox said, "Cut a hole in the ice. Hang your long tail down it. Fish will bite your tail. Wait and you will get many fish."

Bear did this. But his long tail got very cold. It broke off when he pulled it up.

And that's why bears have short tails.

1. What kind of story is this?
   ○ A. folktale   ○ B. poem   ○ C. news story

2. How do you know that Bear once had a long tail?

_____

🌀 BrainTeaser 🌀

Make as many words as you can. Use ONLY the letters in the wheel. Each word must have an **O**, plus two or more letters.

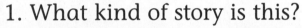

_____

_____

_____

Reading & Math Practice, Grade 1 © 2014 Scholastic Inc.

Number Place

Finish the number line.

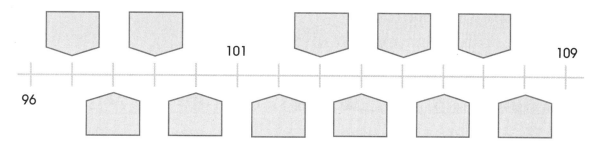

FAST Math

Shade the fractions.

one half   one half   one fourth   one quarter

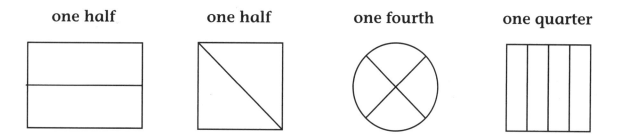

Think Tank

Look at the shape in the first box.
Color the shape where you see it in the row.

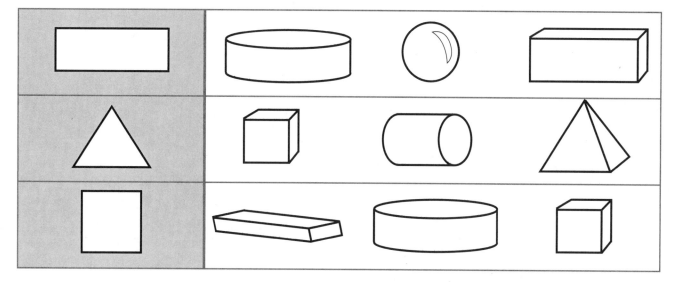

Data Place

Measure the ribbon and pencil.
Use paper clips AND pennies.
Write each length to the nearest unit.

_____ paper clips   _____ pennies

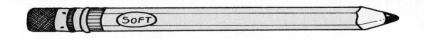

_____ paper clips   _____ pennies

Why does each object have 2 DIFFERENT measurements?

_____

_____

_____

Puzzler

Use number sense.
Figure out each missing digit.

$$
\begin{array}{r}
7\ 5 \\
-\ \boxed{}\ 3 \\
\hline
6\ 2
\end{array}
\qquad
\begin{array}{r}
\boxed{}\ 3 \\
+\ 3\ 6 \\
\hline
8\ 9
\end{array}
\qquad
\begin{array}{r}
\boxed{}\ 9 \\
-\ 1\ 2 \\
\hline
5\ 7
\end{array}
\qquad
\begin{array}{r}
2\ \boxed{} \\
+\ 4\ 1 \\
\hline
7\ 0
\end{array}
$$

Reading & Math Practice, Grade 1 © 2014 Scholastic Inc.

FUN Phonics

Antonyms are opposites. Match each word on the left with its antonym on the right.

old •	• dry
wet •	• fast
thick •	• new
slow •	• smooth
rich •	• poor
bumpy •	• thin

Handwriting Helper

✎ Trace. Then write.

What is your name?

Where is your lunch?

📖 Ready, Set, READ!

Read.
Then answer the questions.

Polar Bears

Polar bears are white. So is the ice where they live. This makes polar bears hard to see. It helps them hunt. They wait for a seal to get near. They grab it with their long claws.

Polar bears stay warm even in icy water. They have two thick layers of fur. Both layers keep the bear warm. The bear also has thick fat under its fur. This helps too.

1. What is it like where polar bears live?
   O A. icy
   O B. dry
   O C. warm

2. What do polar bears eat?

   _____

   _____

   _____

꩜ BrainTeaser ꩜

Make as many words as you can. Use ONLY the letters in the wheel. Each word must have an **I**, plus two or more letters.

_____

_____

_____

Reading & Math Practice, Grade 1 © 2014 Scholastic Inc.

Number Place

Count. Circle tens. Write how many.

_____ tens _____ ones   _____ tens _____ ones

FAST Math

Circle the fraction for the shaded part.

  $\frac{1}{2}$ $\frac{1}{4}$

  $\frac{1}{2}$ $\frac{1}{4}$

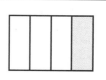 $\frac{1}{2}$ $\frac{1}{4}$

  $\frac{1}{2}$ $\frac{1}{4}$

Think Tank

Eli has 22 marbles.
He keeps 12 of them.
He gives the rest to his
2 sisters. Each gets
the same number.
How many marbles
does each sister get?

_____ marbles each

Show your work
in the tank.

Data Place

Children at a park took a survey. They voted for a favorite summer treat. The table shows the votes.

Use the table to answer the questions.

Summer Treat	Votes
Ice Cream	117
Lemonade	86
Watermelon	71

1. Eighty-six kids voted for _____ .

2. _____ got the most votes.

3. _____ got 71 votes.

4. How many more voted for lemonade than watermelon?

_____

Puzzler

Write a story problem.
Use any numbers from the box.
Be sure you can find the answer.

4	8	11
13	15	20

_____

_____

_____

_____

Reading & Math Practice, Grade 1 © 2014 Scholastic Inc.

Answer Key

Reading 1

Fun Phonics: 1. ball **2.** key **3.** hand **4.** pig **5.** top **6.** web
Handwriting Helper: Check work for accuracy and legibility.
Ready, Set, Read!

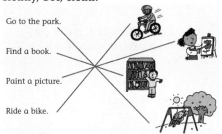

Brainteaser:

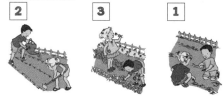

Math 1

Number Place: (Top to bottom) 4, 2; 3, 1, 5
Fast Math: Check child's pictures.
Think Tank: Check child's pictures.
Data Place: star—3, heart—4, moon—2; circle 4
Puzzler:

Reading 2

Fun Phonics: 1. cow **2.** leg **3.** map **4.** duck **5.** pill **6.** fan
Handwriting Helper: Check work for accuracy and legibility.
Ready, Set, Read!

Brainteaser:

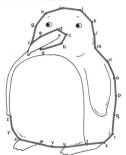

Math 2

Number Place: (Top to bottom) 9, 6; 10, 8, 7
Fast Math: (Left to right) 5, 5, 4; 3, 6, 5
Think Tank: 3, 5, 9, 7
Data Place: (Top to bottom) 6, 7, 5
1. Circle cherry **2.** apples
Puzzler: 3rd hat, 4th bowl, 2nd ladybug

Reading 3

Fun Phonics: 1. salt **2.** game **3.** nest **4.** jeep **5.** vine **6.** zoo
Handwriting Helper: Check work for accuracy and legibility.
Ready, Set, Read!

Brainteaser:

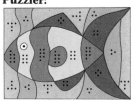

Math 3

Number Place: 2, 3, 5, 6, 7, 9

Fast Math: (Left to right) 7, 8, 9; 7, 10, 9
Think Tank: 3 bats; check child's pictures.
Data Place: 1. 6 **2.** 7 **3.** 9 **4.** 10
Puzzler:

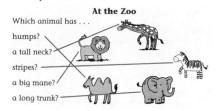

Reading 4

Fun Phonics: 1. crab **2.** leaf **3.** book **4.** broom **5.** soap **6.** bus
Handwriting Helper: Check work for accuracy and legibility.
Ready, Set, Read! (Top to bottom) Tess, Finn, Finn, Tess
Brainteaser:

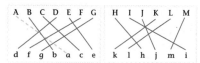

Math 4
Number Place: (Top to bottom) two/2; three/3; four/4; five/5; six/6; seven/7; eight/8; nine/9; ten/10.
Fast Math: 2, 4, 6, 8, 10
Think Tank: 4
Data Place: 1. 5 **2.** 4 **3.** 7 **4.** middle train
Puzzler: 1. 6 **2.** 8 **3.** 7 **4.** 3 **5.** 3 **6.** 1

Reading 5
Fun Phonics: 1. coat **2.** jar **3.** flag **4.** cloud **5.** pool **6.** moon
Handwriting Helper: Check work for accuracy and legibility.
Ready, Set, Read! Hank is the frog in midair; Suzy is swimming in the water.
Brainteaser:

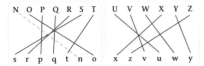

Math 5
Number Place:

      fifth

Fast Math: (Left to right) 6, 7; 8, 9
Think Tank: 2, 4, 7, 9, 10
Data Place: 1. tower of 6 **2.** tower of 3 **3.** 4
Puzzler: Drawings will vary; check child's work.

Reading 6
Fun Phonics: 1. pan **2.** leg **3.** lip **4.** fox **5.** bud **6.** sun
Handwriting Helper: Check work for accuracy and legibility.
Ready, Set, Read! 1. A **2.** Answers will vary; sample answer: big/strong
Brainteaser:

Big	can	You	not	See	kit
old	Dad	tub	Jet	him	May

Math 6
Number Place: 11, 12, 13
Fast Math: sums of 6—3 + 3, 1 + 5, 2 + 4, 4 + 2; sums of 7—5 + 2, 3 + 4, 2 + 5, 1 + 6
Think Tank: 15
Data Place: 2, 2, 1, 2, 10; answers will vary.
Puzzler: 12, 2, 11

Reading 7
Fun Phonics: 1. m **2.** g **3.** b **4.** l **5.** v **6.** n
Handwriting Helper: Check work for accuracy and legibility.
Ready, Set, Read! 1. B **2.** The frog will jump.
Brainteaser:

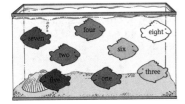

Math 7
Number Place: 14, 15, 16
Fast Math: sums of 8—6 + 2, 1 + 7, 4 + 4, 5 + 3; sums of 9—7 + 2, 3 + 6, 5 + 4, 8 + 1
Think Tank: 8
Data Place: 1. 3 **2.** Kyle **3.** 4
Puzzler: ostrich

Reading 8
Fun Phonics: 1. ham **2.** bag **3.** cap **4.** glass **5.** fan **6.** pad
Handwriting Helper: Check work for accuracy and legibility.
Ready, Set, Read! 1. B **2.** No
Brainteaser: Names—Gus, Nan; Places—hill, sea; Body Words—arm, hip

Math 8
Number Place: 17, 18, 19
Fast Math: 6, 3, 8, 7, 4
Think Tank: 6
Data Place: 1. 4 **2.** Eva **3.** Ming, Jack
Puzzler: 1. 6 **2.** 8 **3.** 10 **4.** Check child's composite shape drawing.

Reading 9
Fun Phonics: 1. cab **2.** crack **3.** lamp **4.** bend **5.** trash **6.** bath
Handwriting Helper: Check work for accuracy and legibility.
Ready, Set, Read! 1. B **2.** two
Brainteaser: Fruits—fig, grapes, plum; Meats—beef, lamb, ham; Drinks—milk, tea, water

Math 9
Number Place:

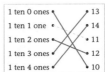 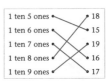

Fast Math: (Left to right) 5, 3, 1; 2, 2, 4
Think Tank: Max, Rob, Kim
Data Place: 1. Monday **2.** 7 **3.** Tuesday
Puzzler: Answers will vary; check child's work.

Reading 10
Fun Phonics: 1. crib **2.** milk **3.** swim **4.** dish **5.** fist **6.** hill
Handwriting Helper: Check work for accuracy and legibility.
Ready, Set, Read! 1. B **2.** Sample answer: It helps you know what to do and in what order.
Brainteaser: -at words—hat, mat, flat; -ip words—lip, trip, dip

Math 10
Number Place: (Top to bottom) 40, 50, 60; 70, 80, 90, 100
Fast Math: (Left to right) 2, 6, 4; 3, 3, 3
Think Tank: 4
Data Place:

Puzzler: (Top to bottom) 1, 2, 4, 3

Reading & Math Practice, Grade 1 © 2014 Scholastic Inc.

Reading 11

Fun Phonics: 1. lick **2.** pin **3.** king **4.** drip **5.** knit **6.** clip
Handwriting Helper: Check work for accuracy and legibility.
Ready, Set, Read! 1. A **2.** Sample answers: You can fly up high; you can look down on things; you feel free.
Brainteaser: -ail words—mail, tail, Gail; -ig words—big, twig, wig

Math 11

Number Place: (Top to bottom) 4, 3; 4, 2, 5
Fast Math: (Left to right) 5, 4, 3; 3, 5, 2
Think Tank: 7
Data Place: 1. 7 **2.** Becky **3.** 9
Puzzler: lines only—E, H, K, V, Z; curves only—O; lines and curves—D, G, J, P, Q, U

Reading 12

Fun Phonics: 1. box **2.** cot **3.** mop **4.** log **5.** sock **6.** pond
Handwriting Helper: Check work for accuracy and legibility.
Ready, Set, Read! 1. A **2.** 1, 3, 5
Brainteaser: -ell words—fell, spell, well; -ot words—dot, spot, not

Math 12

Number Place: (Top to bottom) 58, 94; 71, 49, 26
Fast Math: 9, 3, 9, 5, 1
Think Tank: triangle; check that drawing is an isosceles triangle.
Data Place: 1. 10¢ **2.** ball, yo-yo **3.** bell, yo-yo
Puzzler:

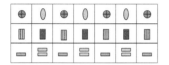

Reading 13

Fun Phonics: 1. rod **2.** stop **3.** fox **4.** frog **5.** knob **6.** clock
Handwriting Helper: Check work for accuracy and legibility.
Ready, Set, Read! 1. A **2.** happy
Brainteaser: -ink words—pink, wink, drink; -ock words—lock, rock, block

Math 13

Number Place: 34, 56, 42
Fast Math: (Left to right) 13, 12, 11; 14, 13, 12
Think Tank: 3
Data Place: 1. 12 **2.** 4 **3.** bananas
Puzzler:

Reading 14

Fun Phonics: 1. tub **2.** bud **3.** mug **4.** sun **5.** bus **6.** hump
Handwriting Helper: Check work for accuracy and legibility.
Ready, Set, Read! 1. A **2.** strong, solid
Brainteaser: Answers may vary; samples include:
-am words—dam, ham, jam, Sam, yam; -op words—bop, cop, hop, mop, pop, stop

Math 14

Number Place: 91, 73, 68
Fast Math: (Left to right) 16, 17, 15; 15, 16, 18
Think Tank: 4
Data Place:

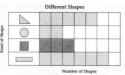

1. 2 **2.** 2 **3.** 16
Puzzler: 56, 12, 16, 51, 19

Reading 15

Fun Phonics: 1. brush **2.** dust **3.** plug **4.** drum **5.** truck **6.** skunk
Handwriting Helper: Check work for accuracy and legibility.
Ready, Set, Read! 1. B **2.** tidy, made, straightened out
Brainteaser: Answers may vary; samples include:
-eed words—deed, feed, reed, seed, weed; -est words—chest, jest, nest, rest, test, west

Math 15

Number Place: (Top to bottom) 5, 3; 6, 8; 4, 9; 7, 0; 2, 5; 3, 1
Fast Math: 12, 18, 14, 16, 10
Think Tank: Check child's drawings; 7
Data Place:

16 coins in all

Puzzler:

Reading 16

Fun Phonics: 1. hen **2.** net **3.** tent **4.** sled **5.** vest **6.** step
Handwriting Helper: Check work for accuracy and legibility.
Ready, Set, Read! 1. A **2.** to keep your brain safe
Brainteaser: 1. bag **2.** fin **3.** sick

Math 16

Number Place:

1	2	3	4	5	6	7	8	9	10
11	12	13	14	15	16	17	18	19	20
21	22	23	24	25	26	27	28	29	30
31	32	33	34	35	36	37	38	39	40

Fast Math: (Left to right) 16, 15; 18, 18
Think Tank: Rob; 3
Data Place:

3 more clocks have numbers only

Puzzler:

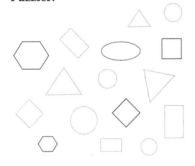

Reading 17

Fun Phonics: 1. belt **2.** shell **3.** check **4.** bench **5.** desk
6. bread
Handwriting Helper: Check work for accuracy and legibility.
Ready, Set, Read! 1. B **2.** A
Brainteaser: Answers will vary; samples include: hop, dog, key, lay, big, dip

Math 17

Number Place: (Left to right) 37, 38, 39; 49, 50, 51; 30, 31, 32; 58, 59, 60
Fast Math: 9, 5, 5, 8, 6
Think Tank: 7
Data Place: 1. 5 **2.** dog **3.** 10 bags
Puzzler:

Reading 18

Fun Phonics: 1. rake **2.** tape **3.** vase **4.** whale **5.** shade
6. skate
Handwriting Helper: Check work for accuracy and legibility.
Ready, Set, Read! 1. B **2.** A
Brainteaser: Answers will vary; samples include: boil, dish, fact, heel, knob, look

Math 18

Number Place: (Left to right) 96, 97, 98; 84, 85, 86; 70, 71, 72; 58, 59, 60
Fast Math: 9, 7, 8, 9, 8
Think Tank: ● □ ●; E = A; ④ ⓪ ⑤
Data Place: 1. 7 **2.** 5 **3.** 2
Puzzler: 18, 19, 16, 19, 14

Reading 19

Fun Phonics: 1. sail **2.** plate **3.** snail **4.** tray **5.** paint **6.** train
Handwriting Helper: Check work for accuracy and legibility.
Ready, Set, Read! 1. gardens **2.** voles **3.** moles
Brainteaser: Answers may vary; most likely choices:
1. o **2.** i **3.** u

Math 19

Number Place: 4, 7; 6, 4; circled sets of ten will vary.
Fast Math: (Left to right) 7, 9, 6; 10, 8, 5
Think Tank: 17
Data Place: 1. (2, 2) **2.** (3, 4) **3.** (4, 1) **4.** Check graph for X at (1, 3).
Puzzler: 1, 6, 1; 64, 74, 84; 24, 27, 30; 20, 30, 25

Reading 20

Fun Phonics: 1. nine **2.** kite **3.** tire **4.** pipe **5.** hike **6.** dime
Handwriting Helper: Check work for accuracy and legibility.
Ready, Set, Read! 1. A **2.** B **3.** Mermaids are not real.
Brainteaser:

Math 20

Number Place: 3 + 3; sixty-four; 87; 2 tens 4 ones
Fast Math: 6, 17, 7, 14, 9, 16
Think Tank: Check that child drew a clock showing 3:00.
Data Place: 1. 6 **2.** 3 **3.** shells **4.** 8
Puzzler: Check child's answers, which may vary.

Reading 21

Fun Phonics: 1. hive **2.** slide **3.** knife **4.** mice **5.** smile **6.** fly
Handwriting Helper: Check work for accuracy and legibility.
Ready, Set, Read! 1. It has no legs. **2.** B
Brainteaser: Check drawing for accuracy and completeness.

Math 21

Number Place: (Left to right) 50, 5, 60; 10, 2, 9
Fast Math: (Left to right) +, −, −; −, +, +
Think Tank: 50
Data Place: 1. 3 **2.** third trip **3.** first trip
Puzzler: numbers < 25—0, 6, 12, 15, 24; numbers 26 to 70—28, 33, 49, 54, 67; numbers > 70—71, 77, 82, 99, 100

Reading 22

Fun Phonics: 1. cone **2.** hole **3.** smoke **4.** hose **5.** crow **6.** fold
Handwriting Helper: Check work for accuracy and legibility.
Ready, Set, Read! 1. B **2.** Four: Bill, Nan, Tom, and Inez
Brainteaser: Check drawing for accuracy and completeness.

Math 22

Number Place: (Left to right) 28, 49, 66; 37, 51, 80
Fast Math: 7, 13, 8, 16
Think Tank: 5
Data Place: 1. 5 **2.** 7 **3.** Circle cookie and donut.
Puzzler: 1. M **2.** S **3.** I **4.** A **5.** T **6.** eighth (or last)

Reading & Math Practice, Grade 1 © 2014 Scholastic Inc.

Reading 23

Fun Phonics: 1. stove **2.** globe **3.** blow **4.** coat **5.** toad **6.** toast
Handwriting Helper: Check work for accuracy and legibility.
Ready, Set, Read! 1. B **2.** 53 Gray Lane
Brainteaser:

J	T	C	A	G	E	L	R
O	I	U	Q	U	A	K	O
S	R	B	N	E	S	T	S
J	E	E	P	M	R	O	E

Math 23

Number Place: (Left to right) 11, 44, 65; 30, 58, 79
Fast Math: (Left to right) 7, 4, 8; 7, 3, 9
Think Tank: 45
Data Place: 2. (2,1) **3.** (4,2) **4.** (3,4)
Puzzler:

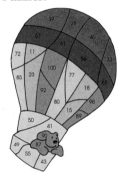

Reading 24

Fun Phonics: 1. mule **2.** fruit **3.** cube **4.** tuba **5.** flute **6.** glue
Handwriting Helper: Check work for accuracy and legibility.
Ready, Set, Read! 1. Glen saw his new house. **2.** B
Brainteaser:

R	O	P	E	K	I	T	H
U	P	A	C	A	K	E	O
B	U	I	S	W	A	N	W
L	A	L	T	K	I	T	E

Math 24

Number Place: (Left to right) 16, 18; 74, 76; 30, 32; 59, 61; 95, 97; 41, 43
Fast Math: 47, 38; circle 47¢
Think Tank: 6
Data Place: only lines—1, 4, 7; only curves—0, 3, 6, 8; lines and curves—2, 5, 9
Puzzler: (Left to right) 5, 4, 11; 10, 8

Reading 25

Fun Phonics: 1. new **2.** dune **3.** ruler **4.** suit **5.** screw **6.** juice
Handwriting Helper: Check work for accuracy and legibility. Answers will vary.
Ready, Set, Read! 1. B **2.** They are too big; they need deep water.
Brainteaser: (Top to bottom) hug/hugs, ring/rings, look/looks, plate/plates

Math 25

Number Place: (Left to right) 28, 29, 30, 31; 49, 50, 51, 52; 77, 78, 79, 80
Fast Math: 8¢, 11¢, 12¢, 10¢, 8¢, 15¢
Think Tank: 24
Data Place: 1. slug **2.** 11 **3.** 3
Puzzler:

Reading 26

Fun Phonics: 1. door **2.** sheep **3.** seed **4.** queen **5.** feet
6. wheel
Handwriting Helper: Check work for accuracy and legibility.
Ready, Set, Read! 1. B **2.** A kitten was stuck in the tree. It was crying for help.
Brainteaser: (Top to bottom) room, floor, step

Math 26

Number Place: (Left to right) >, <, >; >, <, >
Fast Math:

Think Tank: 7, 35
Data Place: Check child's lines; 2, 3, 1
Puzzler: Answers will vary; check that they are reasonable.

Reading 27

Fun Phonics: 1. tea **2.** seal **3.** bean **4.** leash **5.** beak **6.** beads
Handwriting Helper: Check work for accuracy and legibility.
Ready, Set, Read! 1. C **2.** to catch a fish to eat
Brainteaser: 1. peach **2.** fox **3.** kiss **4.** bush

Math 27

Number Place: odd—17, 21, 43, 55; even—6, 10, 38, 44
Fast Math: 46, 93, 67, 74, 85, 59
Think Tank: 34
Data Place:

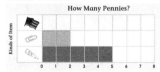

1. 5¢ **2.** 12¢ **3.** 14¢
Puzzler:

▲	▲	▲	▲	▲	▲
☺	⊙	☺	⊙	☺	⊙
⊠	◆	⊠	◆	⊠	◆

Reading 28

Fun Phonics: (Left to right) frame, draw; price, crack, broom
Handwriting Helper: Check work for accuracy and legibility.
Ready, Set, Read! 1. B **2.** Answers will vary; check child's response.
Brainteaser: 1. sleeps **2.** flies. Answers will vary for 3 and 4; samples include: **3.** crawls, moves **4.** laughs, smiles, grins

Math 28
Number Place: (Left to right) 15, 20, 25, 30, 35, 45, 50, 55, 60, 65, 70, 80, 85, 90, 95
Fast Math: 35, 88, 46, 51, 63, 74
Think Tank:

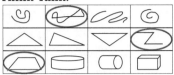

Data Place:

Puzzler:

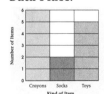

Reading 29
Fun Phonics: (Left to right) plane, sleep; blast, globe, flag
Handwriting Helper: Check work for accuracy and legibility.
Ready, Set, Read! 1. Sample answer: It tells you that you get some water from what you eat. **2.** A
Brainteaser: (Left to right) jump, rib, shoe; flat, much, when

Math 29
Number Place: (Left to right) 20, 30, 40, 50, 60, 70, 80, 90
Fast Math: 74, 88, 91, 82, 77, 99
Think Tank: 111
Data Place:

What Kids Do Before Bed

1. 4 **2.** 14
Puzzler: 1. 12¢ **2.** 10¢ **3.** 14¢ **4.** 13¢

Reading 30
Fun Phonics: (Left to right) snug, steam or stream, space, smile, scoot
Handwriting Helper: Check work for accuracy and legibility.
Ready, Set, Read! 1. C **2.** because she loves food
Brainteaser: (Left to right) line, run, start; boot, horse, ride

Math 30
Number Place: (Left to right) 80, 70, 60, 50, 40, 30, 20, 10
Fast Math: 25, 22, 11, 34, 28, 19
Think Tank: 77
Data Place:

Darla found 14 items in all.

Puzzler: Pictures may vary; check child's drawings.

Reading 31
Fun Phonics: 1. hand/nd **2.** fact/ct **3.** child/ld **4.** mask/sk
5. stump/mp **6.** belt/lt
Handwriting Helper: Check work for accuracy and legibility.
Ready, Set, Read! 1. A **2.** to get bigger and turn blue
Brainteaser: (Top to bottom) 3-2-1; 3-1-2; 2-3-1; 2-1-3

Math 31
Number Place: (Left to right) 19, 56, 64; 38, 97, 75
Fast Math: 4:00, 7:00, 10:00, 1:00
Think Tank: 53
Data Place:

1. 6 **2.** apples, bananas

Puzzler:

Reading 32
Fun Phonics: 1. wasp/sp **2.** bird/rd **3.** fork/rk **4.** skunk/nk
5. fist/st **6.** paint/nt
Handwriting Helper: Check work for accuracy and legibility.
Ready, Set, Read! 1. to learn how to swim **2.** B
Brainteaser:

Math 32
Number Place: (Left to right) 3, 64, 88; 51, 75, 62
Fast Math:

2:00   6:00   11:00

Think Tank: 50
Data Place:

Puzzler:

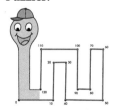

216

Reading 33

Fun Phonics: 1. thirty **2.** shirt **3.** chicken **4.** shut **5.** chop **6.** think
Handwriting Helper: Check work for accuracy and legibility.
Ready, Set, Read! 1. C **2.** Marc Brown and his son
Brainteaser: 1. fox **2.** ant **3.** frog. **4.** hen **5.** duck **6.** pig

Math 33

Number Place: (Top to bottom) twenty/20; forty/40; sixty/60; eighty/80; hundred/100; thirty/30; fifty/50; seventy/70; ninety/90
Fast Math: 12:30, 4:30, 8:30, 2:30
Think Tank: 4 dimes + 2 nickels
Data Place: 1. 7 **2.** 3 **3.** 2 **4.** Sunny **5.** Tuesday, Friday
Puzzler: (Left to right) 43, 48, 46; 84, 74, 79

Reading 34

Fun Phonics: 1. wheels **2.** phone **3.** When **4.** there **5.** photo **6.** this
Handwriting Helper: Check work for accuracy and legibility.
Ready, Set, Read! 1. C **2.** red, white, and blue
Brainteaser: 1. black **2.** brown **3.** green **4.** blue **5.** yellow **6.** pink

Math 34

Number Place: (Left to right) 2, 3; 4, 6; 8, 9
Fast Math:

10:30   5:30   9:00

Think Tank: Pam
Data Place: Answers will vary; check that answers on chart are reasonable.
Puzzler: Answers will vary; check child's drawings and patterns.

Reading 35

Fun Phonics: 1. king **2.** ring **3.** fang **4.** wing **5.** long **6.** sing
Handwriting Helper: Check work for accuracy and legibility.
Ready, Set, Read! 1. C **2.** They can sting you.
Brainteaser: 1. fact **2.** fiction **3.** fiction **4.** fact

Math 35

Number Place: (Left to right) 20, 30, 60, 80; 40, 70, 80, 90
Fast Math: 56, 77, 99, 79, 77, 87
Think Tank: 8:00
Data Place: Check child's lines; 2, 1, 3
Puzzler: 32, 64

Reading 36

Fun Phonics: 1. couch **2.** cash **3.** tooth **4.** wash **5.** month **6.** punch
Handwriting Helper: Check work for accuracy and legibility.
Ready, Set, Read! 1. B **2.** The fly said please.
Brainteaser: Answers will vary; check that child's sentences are reasonable.

Math 36

Number Place: (Left to right) 4, 4, 7; 5, 8, 9
Fast Math: 50, 30, 80; 20, 60, 80; 60, 20, 80
Think Tank: 13
Data Place:

	Ducks	Swans	Total
Roscoe	16	3	**19**
Noah	17	**5**	22
Kerry	**13**	6	19

1. 17 **2.** Kerry **3.** 19 **4.** Kerry
Puzzler:

2	1	4	3
4	**3**	**2**	1
1	**2**	**3**	4
3	4	1	2

Reading 37

Fun Phonics: 2. licking, licked **3.** planting, planted **4.** brushing, brushed **5.** spelling, spelled **6.** playing, played
Handwriting Helper: Check work for accuracy and legibility.
Ready, Set, Read! 1. C **2.** wax
Brainteaser: Questions will vary; check that child's questions are reasonable.

Math 37

Number Place: (Left to right) 20, 20, 50, 70; 30, 50, 70, 90
Fast Math: 50, 30, 20; 70, 30, 40; 90, 10, 80
Think Tank: (Top to bottom) Friday, Monday, Saturday, Sunday, Tuesday, Thursday, Wednesday; 6, 2, 7, 1, 3, 5, 4
Data Place: 1. $5 **2.** small popcorn + large soda or large popcorn + small soda **3.** $20
Puzzler: 24, 28, 42, 48, 82, 84

Reading 38

Fun Phonics: 2. mixing, mixed **3.** reaching, reached **4.** parting, parted **5.** needing, needed **6.** jumping, jumped
Handwriting Helper: Check work for accuracy and legibility.
Ready, Set, Read! 1. C **2.** So Chet could take them home.
Brainteaser: Sentences will vary; check that child's sentences are reasonable.

Math 38

Number Place: 5, 5; 6, 9; 7, 7
Fast Math: 31, 62, 12, 72, 40, 23
Think Tank: 43, 32, 21
Data Place:

Books Taken Out

Jamila	■ ■ ■			
Opal	■ ■ ■ ■ ■			
Riley	■ ■ ■ ■			

Key: ■ = 1 book

Puzzler:

53	48	51	43	57		
50	46	49	51	23		
51	45	44	49	15		
43	42	63	65	7	11	93
39	41	40	31	53	13	6	1	3
37	38	35	23	11	8	5	4	2
36	26	24	22	21	9	10		
34	28	25	20	15	13	12		
32	30	23	18	16	14	11		

Reading 39
Fun Phonics: 2. older, oldest **3.** taller, tallest **4.** higher, highest
5. younger, youngest
Handwriting Helper: Check work for accuracy and legibility.
Ready, Set, Read! 1. C **2.** three
Brainteaser: Answers will vary; check that the sentences make sense.

Math 39
Number Place: 55, 67, 70; 55, 62, 66; 49, 50, 94; 75, 104, 118
Fast Math: 70, 70, 50, 90, 60, 80
Think Tank: 5
Data Place:

Vicki's Veggies

Veggie	Tally	Number
Carrots	IIII	4
Peppers	HHI I	6 .
Potatoes	HHI HHI	10

1. potatoes **2.** carrots **3.** 20
Puzzler: 19; 65; 75

Reading 40
Fun Phonics: 1. sunflower **2.** doghouse **3.** flashlight
4. scarecrow **5.** wheelchair
Handwriting Helper: Check work for accuracy and legibility.
Ready, Set, Read! 1. B **2.** Gus
Brainteaser: (Left to right) butterfly, snowflake

Math 40
Number Place: 41, 33, 28; 59, 49, 39; 83, 38, 33; 117, 105, 99
Fast Math: 69, 50, 70, 44, 77, 60
Think Tank: Answers may vary; check child's drawings.
Data Place:

Brushstrokes for Lizzy

Monday						
Tuesday						
Wednesday						
Thursday						
Friday						

0 10 20 30 40 50 60
Number of Brushstrokes

difference between most and least strokes is 30

Puzzler: (Left to right) F, H, F; H, F, H; H, H, F

Reading 41
Fun Phonics: 1. ladybug **2.** bathrobe **3.** birdcage **4.** sailboat
5. popcorn **6.** starfish
Handwriting Helper: Check work for accuracy and legibility.
Ready, Set, Read! 1. B **2.** to keep water out of the inside of the car
Brainteaser: (Left to right) mailbox, grasshopper

Math 41
Number Place: (Left to right) 33, 86; 75, 41; 99, 15
Fast Math: 32, 53, 58, 34, 12, 49
Think Tank: Answers may vary; sample answer:
3 dimes, 2 nickels, 1 penny
Data Place:

Books Read	Tally	Number of People
0	II	2
1	HHI I	6
2	HHI IIII	9
3	HHL	5

1. 2 **2.** 6 **3.** 2
Puzzler: 1. 71 **2.** 97 **3.** 15 **4.** 24

Reading 42
Fun Phonics: 1. backpack **2.** raincoat **3.** cupcake **4.** lunchbox
5. airplane. **6.** football
Handwriting Helper: Check work for accuracy and legibility.
Ready, Set, Read! 1. B **2.** Worms live in soil.
Brainteaser: 1. ? **2.** ! **3.** ? **4.** !

Math 42
Number Place: (Left to right) 39, 28, 43; 64, 17, 52; 46, 100, 71
Fast Math: 33, 34, 40, 51, 75, 22
Think Tank: 6
Data Place: 1. ring toss **2.** face painting **3.** 3 **4.** 9
Puzzler:

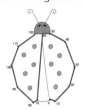

Reading 43
Fun Phonics: (Top to bottom) She is/She's; It is/It's;
We are/We're; You are/You're; They are/They're
Handwriting Helper: Check work for accuracy and legibility.
Ready, Set, Read! 1. C **2.** They hook their legs together.
Brainteaser: Answers will vary; check that child's words fit the rules.

Math 43
Number Place: (Left to right) <, >, <; >, >, <
Fast Math: 41, 98, 50, 78, 89, 22
Think Tank: 30
Data Place:

First Graders at Moss School

Class	Girls	Boys	Total
1A	13	14	27
1B	14	14	28
1C	14	13	27

1. 1B **2.** 1A **3.** 27 students
Puzzler: (Top to bottom) I, U, O; O, A, E

Reading 44
Fun Phonics: (Top to bottom) He will/He'll; It will/It'll;
We will/We'll; You will/You'll; They will/They'll
Handwriting Helper: Check work for accuracy and legibility.
Ready, Set, Read! 1. B **2.** ice cream
Brainteaser: 1. It is hot and dry. **2.** My apple is too soft.

Math 44
Number Place: less than 20—0, 8, 12, 17; between 21 and
50—26, 31, 39, 40, 48; greater than 50—63, 77, 81, 86, 89, 95
Fast Math: 31, 60, 89, 21, 90, 30
Think Tank: 9
Data Place: jeans only—Ben, Dawn, Henry; glasses only—
Ann, Carl, Gina; both—Ella, Fritz
Puzzler: 8, 16, 9

Reading 45
Fun Phonics: 1. isn't **2.** don't **3.** aren't **4.** can't **5.** doesn't
Handwriting Helper: Check work for accuracy and legibility.
Ready, Set, Read! 1. B **2.** itchy
Brainteaser: (Left to right) yell, goofy, fast; noise, same, center

Reading & Math Practice, Grade 1 © 2014 Scholastic Inc.

Math 45

Number Place: (Top to bottom) 7, 2; 8, 9; 2, 4; 9, 0; 6, 3; 3, 1
Fast Math: 60, 20, 80; 30, 50, 80; 40, 40, 80
Think Tank: 7
Data Place:

Child	Letters in First Name	Letters in Last Name	Total Number of Letters
Vara	9	11	20
Anna	9	12	21
Tala	10	9	19

1. Tala **2.** Anna **3.** Anna
Puzzler: Both lines are the same length, but the arrows make one look longer than the other.

Reading 46

Fun Phonics: Pairs 2, 3, 6, 7, and 9 rhyme.
Handwriting Helper: Check work for accuracy and legibility.
Ready, Set, Read! 1. B **2.** C
Brainteaser: (Left to right) happy, slow, asleep; sit, fix, pull

Math 46

Number Place: (Left to right) 74, 45, 81; 67, 98, 56; 25, 82, 57; 4, 33, 48
Fast Math: 60, 30, 30; 80, 50, 30; 90, 60, 30
Think Tank: 15
Data Place: 1. jungle gym **2.** seesaw **3.** swing **4.** 16
Puzzler: 1. stapler **2.** chair **3.** boot **4.** bus

Reading 47

Fun Phonics: short *a*—flat, track; long *a*—brain, grape; short *i*—click, pill; long *i*—mile, shine
Handwriting Helper: Check work for accuracy and legibility.
Ready, Set, Read! 1. C **2.** high
Brainteaser: Answers will vary; check child's sentences.

Math 47

Number Place: Answers will vary; check for accuracy.
Fast Math: (Left to right) 4 + 7 = 47; 12 – 6 = 18; 20 – 10 = 30
Think Tank: Check child's drawing; fourths means having 4 equal pieces.
Data Place:

Letter	Tally	Number
a	|	1
b	|	1
d	||||	4
e	||||	4
f	||	2
r	||	2
t	||	1

Puzzler: 1. pitcher **2.** bathtub **3.** bucket **4.** teapot

Reading 48

Fun Phonics: short *e*—edge, test; long *e*—dream, seen; short *o*—blond, flock; long *o*—roast, whole
Handwriting Helper: Check work for accuracy and legibility.
Ready, Set, Read! 1. B **2.** It's too hot during the day.
Brainteaser: Answers will vary; check that the words include *e* and two more letters, and are spelled correctly.

Math 48

Number Place: 78, 79, 80, 81; 50, 51, 52, 53; 99, 100, 101, 102
Fast Math: (Left to right) 14, 10, 8; 10, 5, 22
Think Tank: 10 + 0, 9 + 1, 8 + 2, 7 + 3, 6 + 4, 5 + 5
Data Place: 1. Tuesday, January 27 **2.** 5 **3.** 44 inches **4.** less
Puzzler: 1. equal **2.** hundred **3.** number **4.** quarter **5.** twenty **6.** zero

Reading 49

Fun Phonics: (Top to bottom) pick/choose; drag/pull; jump/leap; fix/mend; story/tale
Handwriting Helper: Check work for accuracy and legibility.
Ready, Set, Read! 1. A **2.** The story tells us, and the long tail broke off.
Brainteaser: Answers will vary; check that the words include *o* and two more letters, and are spelled correctly.

Math 49

Number Place:

96 [97] [99] 101 [103] [105] [107] 109
      [98] [100] [102] [104] [106] [108]

Fast Math: Check child's shadings.
Think Tank: rectangular prism; pyramid; cube
Data Place: Answers may vary because the measuring tools are different sizes; check that the answers are reasonable.
Puzzler: 1, 5, 6, 9

Reading 50

Fun Phonics: (Top to bottom) wet/dry; thick/thin; slow/fast; rich/poor; bumpy/smooth
Handwriting Helper: Check work for accuracy and legibility.
Ready, Set, Read! 1. A **2.** seals
Brainteaser: Answers will vary; check that the words include *i* and two more letters, and are spelled correctly.

Math 50

Number Place: 7, 8; 9, 0; circled sets of ten will vary.
Fast Math: $\frac{1}{4}, \frac{1}{2}, \frac{1}{4}, \frac{1}{2}$
Think Tank: 5
Data Place: 1. lemonade **2.** ice cream **3.** watermelon **4.** 15
Puzzler: Check child's problem and answer.

You can use this page to work out your answers.

You can use this page to work out your answers.

You can use this page to work out your answers.

You can use this page to work out your answers.

You can use this page to work out your answers.

Reading & Math Practice, Grade 1 © 2014 Scholastic Inc.